I killed Bin Laden

The wildest dance of the history

Mehdi Rezaei

Treanslated By Manda kia

mehdi_rezayi_mehdi@yahoo.com

Title: I killed Bin Laden
Subtitle: The wildest dance of the history
Author: Mehdi Rezaei
Translator: Manda kia
Cover Design: Ali Khiabanian
ISBN-13: 978-1939123961
Published by Supreme Century, USA
Printed in the United State of America

Albert Einstein :

The world is a dangerous place to live

Not because of the people who are evil

But because of the people who don't do anything about it

Aida Majid Abadi :

Tune your hands

Let's get ready

For the wildest dance of the history

I killed Bin Laden

Jones says, "Come on David. Come and see what a new play these rascals have schemed!"

I say, "What are you talking about?"

Jones says, "TV news...let me turn it up."

I enter the room. Now I can hear it clearly. I am staring at the TV with my hands on my waist.

"Robert O'Neal the ex-commando who was in Pakistan for participating in the mission concerning killing the ex-leader of Al-Qaeda said to Washington Post in a new interview that it was his shot that killed Bin Laden.

His claim defies Matt Bissonnette's utterance. Matt Bissonnette is the other commando who took part at the same mission. In a book in 2012, he claimed that Bin Laden was killed by his shot."

I say, "Please shut it up. What do you think about the new play that they have schemed?"

Jones says, "Well, you damn guy, they are afraid of us. The United States paid through the nose and a heavy price for what you did. US planned this scheme by his best writers and intellectuals and then you shit the biggest and most costly scenario of the history. You changed that historical scenario. They want to pull us out of our closet by the new claims through the reports and media or they want just to say that it has been a repeated unreal claim by many nuts if we reveal the truth once."

It has been a long time that something inside me has been titillating my curiosity to ask this question and just Jones knows the answer to this question. So I ask, "Was killing Saddam enjoyable for you?"

Jones says, "I have never enjoyed killing. Never, even Saddam. But I have no doubt that I did right."

I say, "In fact you ruined their plan so they made that ridiculous televised hanging."

Jones says, "Not important. We must do our job. Then they can scheme any plan they wish. What is of high importance is that we ruined the key play."

Tony Bear says, "Hey you damn bastards! I also killed Gaddafi, but I don't disturb other people's sleeping. Shit your bed and shut your eyes. We have a big job tomorrow; a bigger job than killing Bin Laden, Saddam and Gaddafi. So shut up."

Episode One

A dirty job stays dirty until there isn't a good reason for justifying it. When we see someone is doing something dirty, we might think of ourselves, "What a dirty bastard guy." But wait, we shouldn't judge soon. What you see is not always the whole story. You might say that the dirty bastard guy is right if you know the truth about him. You might even persuade him and say hey buddy, beat a shit out of him! Fuck him.

It is a truth. Am I right? You want to say, no, but the word," yes" is twinkling in your mind, isn't it? Ok, no problem. But stay with me to the end of this story. We would have many disagreements in this story. Not important. Disagreement is a good thing but in case it is between two logical men. Because those two logical men sit, think and resolve the problem. Although they might have a lot of discussions and wrangles but they reach a conclusion in the end anyway.

I describe you a scene. Then tell me what your idea is about it. Once I got someone in a trap within a cellar of a desolate house. Then I stripped him thoroughly. Be sure that it wasn't a woman. I never rape a woman, even if I hate her. I hate such an act and more I hate those who do this. It was a Black. But you must know that I am not also a raciest. Although I am a White but I respect all human beings with any kind of skin color and race. I respect any human being, oh...human being...what a simple and complicated word.

I fixed him to the wall by rope with open arms and open legs like an X. Then I plugged in a cutting machine. Definitely you know what kind of cutting machine I mean. Those ones which easily cut solid objects like stones and halve them. I kept the cutting machine close to his testicles between his legs and gazed into his eyes. He was frightened. He couldn't believe I did that. I didn't believe myself. My whole body was overwhelmed with weird heat. Cold sweat broke out on his whole body. The sweat was so much that was dropping down on the floor. He was shivering as if high voltage electricity was passng through his body. When he got sure that I was decisive, he said breathlessly, "swear...swear to God...you are making...a mistake. You are...making...a mistake."

You can't imagine how that dirty pig was begging. But I didn't feel pity for him. What about you? I hope you don't want to say that you feel pity for someone whom I was doing such a damn thing with. Me? In no way, I didn't feel pity for him at all. Even a little. I didn't feel pity for anyone no more. I became like a stone. I am sure you say to yourself that now the dirty guy who is describing these things is one of those who was afflicted with misfortune during the exchange of drugs and now he wants to kick a shit out of him with the aim of deterring others to reach his goal.

Don't judge immediately. Two issues are clear until now. First of all what I did wasn't a sexual raping or a racism act. It wasn't also a private retaliation for money or drug or a girl whom I died for out of love. No, what I did was more important. Although I can't, with these justifications, wipe out the shit feature that you have made out of what I am in your mind, but it isn't important. You don't have to keep on with me anymore. Close it...close this book and mind your own business. So why aren't you still reading this? Why are you still keeping on? Do you want to keep on with me to see why I did such a thing? That's ok so come on.

I was gazing at him for some seconds and didn't say anything then I behaved in a way that I was more decisive to cut his eggs from the bottom by the cutting machine. In fact I was really going to do that. He shouted loudly, "Swear to all the sacred...swear...I swear that you are making a mistake."

I gazed at him again and thought that what were really those sacred things that he was talking about? It wasn't that I didn't know what they were but I don't know why people go after sacred things just when they are afflicted with unluckiness and misfortune. Most of us call God and the sacred just when it is too late.

I gazed at him and said, "Son of a bitch, do you really know what the sacred is?"

By saying the words, "son of a bitch", my father was reminded to me. Don't think in a bad way. My father wasn't a bastard. He was too good in fact. I remembered him because he was always telling me, "If once someone kills me, you have no right to call him a bastard because you stigmatize his parents by saying that. It is a big stigmatization because it means that the man was a child born to unmarried parents so by saying this you don't stigmatize him; you stigmatize his mother and father and stigmatization is a big sin."

Of course he said all this with love and affection after slapping me sharply on my ears. I was about ten or twelve. I was playing football with my neighbor's boy in front of my house. I don't remember exactly the words which were exchanged between us but I shouted, "Hey bastard, give me my ball."

It was just some seconds after I had mentioned the word that my father opened the door. He came towards me with long and fast steps and slapped me on my ears so sharply that I fell on the ground. I didn't know the meaning of bastard before the night of that day in which it happened to me and I wondered why my father behaved me like that. But that night before the dinner, my father explained what that word meant and after that I never ever repeated that word again.

Of course I never said it again until I fixed him to the wall and said," Son of a bitch, do you really know what the sacred is? And again, I hated myself for saying that word. Why did I insult his parents for his dirty jobs?"

He averted his face away from me. He was crying. I knew that he didn't like to cry like that. But when your hands and feet are fastened and an angry man is in front of you with a cutting machine that is moving around your genital organ between your legs or any other part of your body, can you do anything else except crying in such a situation? For example, can you smile and say that oh my dear, please don't make a joke!? Or for example, can you say that you are such a funny guy!? Or I don't know...the other expressions like these ones!?

Of course I was too angry and wild that he couldn't even think of saying statements like those. Although I was too angry but there was a smile on my lips and if someone had seen us in that situation, he would have thought it was a ridiculous fun. But I was deadly serious and that dirty guy could thoroughly understand what my smile meant.

I said, "Ok, now that I am wrong – tell me where my mistake is. Tell me what the true story is. Tell me a logical reason for all those happenings and stories to convince me I am wrong."

He looked at me and said, "What must I say? I was a piece like you. All of us did our duty as they ordered us."

I said, "Yes...yes...we were all pieces – pieces for giving services, pieces for defense. But we didn't defend people in there while everything could terminate well with our interference. But why didn't we do that?"

"Well...well, you see, you understand me too. Yes...you understand me...well I was a piece like you. You...why didn't you keep on with the operation?"

"Because you ordered for withdrawal."

"Completely right. Well...well...you tell me, why did I order for withdrawal?"

"Because someone ordered you, on walkie-talkie, for withdrawal. "

"Well...well...damn guy, I mean the same. We must all abide by the commander's order. You obeyed me and I obeyed my commander. "

"That's all right. You were a piece like me. But tell me who ordered you for withdrawal?"

"Oh my God, it was a secret operation. Don't talk in a way that you don't know what a secret operation is."

I smiled and asked, "So secret that it hasn't been recorded in any document of the organization!? Even in the secret documents section!? No, I can't accept it. In fact the very issue encouraged me to find why the operation took place, why it was stopped and who ordered the command for stopping the operation. That is right that we were both pieces within the operation but our roles were different.

You were the commander of the operation. You received the commands and conveyed them so you surely know who ordered the command for stopping the operation and why?"

These things...are none of our business...we are soldiers and must do our duty...we must just obey.

He was talking in a way that I felt he was still playing the role of a commander and I had to remind him that he was my captive. I pressed the cutting machine on the upper muscle of his leg for a moment and then took it back. His eyes opened wider and his mouth got open as wide as was possible. He opened his mouth and shouted loudly, so loudly that I had never heard such a loud cry. Now he was sure that I wasn't joking. His leg was cut at the size of a span. I got my head nearer to his leg. I could see his leg bone. He became listless and the pain of the rupture was surely making him crazy and I enjoyed torturing him.

How terrible it is when you reach the point of barbarianism and you enjoy either torturing a man or watching a man who is tortured. But the issue is that you yourself don't like to be barbarian but they are others who make a barbarian guy out of you. They don't know what they do with the soul and spirit of others and after making such wild people out of them, they themselves are afraid of them and say, "Oh my God, why do they become like this? Why do they go so wild?"

The blood was shedding down to the floor sliding beneath his foot. I got up and looked for something among the waste matters around in there and found a band and fasten it around the upper part of his leg where it was cut in order to stop bleeding. I didn't want him to die; I wanted to reach a conclusion. In spite of my barbarian behavior, the smile wasn't fading out of my lips and it isn't a lie to say that I was enjoying watching that dirty guy in that situation. Yes, I enjoyed. It was a truth. I...enjoyed and how sorrowful it was!

Now you are definitely telling yourself that well, this is one of those dirty and bastard guys who enjoy torturing others; a psycho...an ill person...a full-scale brutal guy...a mother-born murderer. But no, it isn't like this. I am such a guy or it is better to say that I was such a guy that the slightest shape of hurting others made me crazy. For example, once I saw, in the street, a father who was repeatedly slapping sharply his little son. I went towards him and held him tightly by his collars and smashed him to the wall in a way that he couldn't breathe well.

I liked to smash his nose. I liked to break his arm in a way that he couldn't slap his son anymore. I looked at the boy's face for a moment. I saw both happiness and sadness on his face. Of course it might be just my perception of his facial expression but I saw both of them on his face. On one hand he was happy because someone was found to release him out of his father's slaps and on the other hand he was sad because someone grappled his father.

I smashed him to the wall and he was astonished with my reaction. My behavior was so weird to him that he didn't dare to say anything and by seeing my muscular arms, he didn't also dare to have a slightest move. I clenched my fist and brought it close to my ear. It was ready to go on his face and my look moved frequently between the man's eyes and the boy. I let go of his collars and said, "If you slap him once more, I will break your hand. Believe me I do it; don't doubt."

While he was astonished with what had happened, he took his son's hand and went away. By each movement of taking four or five steps forward, the boy turned back and smiled at me. A child's smile! Oh my God! How beautiful is a child's smile! A child's sweet smile. Have you ever seen it? Don't say that well, I am not blind; I have seen many times. But pay attention! A child's smile is one of the most beautiful things that can clear up your mind out of this issue that how much this world is dirty. But just things like this that might seem apparently of tiny importance are able to make you hopeful in this world which has been filled with many dirty things. They can tell you, "Hey guy, this world has also pretty things. Open your eyes! Look well!" But just now I have no other choice but to tell you about the dirty things of this world.

I asked, "Who commanded for withdrawal? Why are you taking me for a ride? I accept that you were just a piece but when you don't say who the head of the operation was, I am sure that you were also a part of this dirty play."

He tried to keep his head up in order to talk face to face but he became listless and couldn't have the control of his head that was bent down.

He said, "no...no...I was just a piece...a servant...a man of generosity...a soldier."

By hearing the very last words, I lost my control and pressed, without thinking, the cutting machine into the middle of his legs. Blood splashed to my face. I stood up and threw away the cutting machine. I restlessly fisted him on his nose, on his teeth, on his eyes and on his jaw. I didn't see anything but blood. For a moment, I was frightened by what I was doing. I looked at my bloody hands and the blood that was shedding down from his head, face and the middle of his legs.

He was dying and it wasn't important for me at all. He had a wife and a child but it wasn't also important for me. The absence of the dirty guys like him is more valuable than their presence; even for their wives and children. I wasn't a nut or a murderer and am not also now. But through searching, I found that the operation was a separate one from the other organization's entire secret operations. The secret operation?! Now I was doubtful about all operations in which I took part. Who knows all those operations were urgent?

Yes, I killed a man. Man?! Oh...man. What a simple and complicated word!

Before killing him, I had performed a hidden researching and entered the intelligence networks of the organization. I was sure that all operations even a secret one had to be recorded somewhere within the archive of the organization. Despite of all those endeavors and researches which could bring about troubles for me, I couldn't find the so-called document, T2. We were fifty soldiers in the operations. I studied all fifty operation participants' files and I found that the operation days were recorded as off days for all of us in them. I explain you all those happenings because I want you to know that what I did had a reason and wasn't out of delusion.

Of course if the forty nine other soldiers like me were witness of all those events in that operation, we all together might be after the whys. But it was just me who observed what happened. I could close my eyes to all those events and go and take a walk. Of course it might have been better to do that. Look around yourself. People close their eyes easily. They don't care. You can avert your look, close your eyes and think of something else. Then you say to yourself, "Go to hell! It's none of your business. You are fine and have no problem." And it is the most ridiculous feature of man.

But I couldn't because I wasn't a sort of man who could close his eyes. That was why I entered the organization. I came to be the soldier of United Nations in spite of all dangers. I became the peace soldier of the organization. I accepted to pass the most harsh and difficult trainings in order to be one of the best forces. But exactly when we could be useful, a foolish act took place and they ordered for withdrawal and stopped the operation – an order which raised a catastrophe and a catastrophe which I was witness of all its moments.

I was gazing at his cold contracted dead body for some minutes. The sound of the last drops of his blood shedding down on the floor was irritating like the pound of beating a sledgehammer on the iron. It was my folly. I lost the only available piece due to my foolish act. I hated myself not for killing him or enjoying torturing him to death. I hated myself because I lost him, by not controlling my nerves, without prizing right information out of him. Of course the reason which encouraged me to kill him might be that I couldn't succeed to pump him for a right name or information. Formerly I also tried a lot to pump other top brass for getting information about the reason of stopping the T2 operation and that was why they became suspicious of me for my questions or for my request to transfer me from the operation section to the intelligence section.

Well, now tell me your idea about it. Are you still thinking that I am a dirty guy? Really? I told you before that don't judge soon. You might be later ashamed of yourself for thinking about me like this. But it was just the beginning; a very simple and normal beginning. Now I am going to tell you things that are so much dirtier and more ridiculous than those events.

You might tell me that I didn't have to kill the commander. I could identify him and pump him for information. I did it before but it took me to nowhere. When I couldn't analyze those events, I went to see Major Jones. Of course he got retired some months before the operation. I didn't reach any conclusion after some months researching and I decided to see him. Before getting retired, he was my direct commander and also a friend out of working time. We sometimes drank coffee or had a drink together on the nights when we were both off.

When he opened the door and saw me, he petrified for a moment and said, "Hey David! What are you doing here man? Nice to see you."

He hugged me. In those days in which we were practicing military trainings, he was like a rabid dog that you didn't dare to get near. I was directly working under his surveillance within the last five years of his military services. He had an unexpected retirement and it was too difficult for me to accept it. In the evening, we were chatting together after finishing daily military practicing. We were talking about the world events; about the wars and blood shedding. About the issue that how is difficult to bear this dirty world. He used to put his hand on my shoulder and say," We accepted to encounter danger in order to clear the world out of dirt for people. Never forget it."

His retirement was sooner than the due time and he himself requested for it. I asked him many times for the reason to make such a decision but his answers weren't convincing and he said he wanted to spend more time at home. I liked him and I missed him. His retirement became a good excuse for me to go to meet him after a couple of months. When I saw him, he seemed older and more withered than before. His hair all became white while he wasn't more than fifty five.

His wife asked loudly from inside the house, "Jones! Do we have a guest?"

"My friend David Darabont."

"Well, guide him to come in."

With a head gesture, he pointed at his wife and said, "You see how much she is kind. Come in. let's have a drink."

I entered the house. I saw his wife who was sitting on a wheelchair. By seeing me, she smiled and said, "Hello Mr. Darabont. You are welcome."

I didn't expect to see Jones's wife in that condition at all. He never told me about this issue and never complained about it. His wife's hair was also entirely white as if it has been white in all her life. I stammered, "Sss...sorry... I don't...really want to take...your time now...I made a prompt decision..."

He put his hand on my shoulder and said, "No problem. You are welcome. Nice to meet you."

He directed me, by gesture, to have a seat and went to the kitchen. His wife turned, her wheelchair which was facing the television, towards me. Then she turned the TV down and said, "With those well-built muscles, you must be one of Jones's colleagues. Aren't you?"

"Yes, of course ex-colleague."

Jones shouted from the kitchen," Please Liza, please, stop talking about people's attractive muscles. You are still holding fast to people's attractive muscles at this age. You must be ashamed of yourself. Our hair is white."

Liza laughed and said, "You are pulling my leg! It was you that was holding fast to people's muscles. Did you forget?"

Jones came out of the kitchen with a dish of fruits and put it on the table. He faced me and said, "Do you know how I fell in love with Liza?"

Liza laughed and said," Damn guy! That's enough. That's enough."

"Let me tell him, Liza. Don't make a joke out of it. We never had a child and I always liked to tell this story for my children. Now we take him as our child."

Liza said, "Damn you Jones. Damn you. Stop it."

She said this and suppressed her laughing face with her hands.

He gestured me with his hand and said, "Don't care her. Let her say anything as she wishes."

Liza was looking down as she was shy and suppressed her face with her hands.

Jones continued," Liza and I both worked in the organization. We both practiced at the organization gym every afternoon. I wanted to have a closer tie with her but I couldn't find any excuses for it."

Liza and I burst into laughter. Jones was very excited in the beginning of his talks but then his excitement started to subside. I felt his eyes were filled with tears for a moment. He looked at Liza and said, "Liza was really beautiful... attractive...and fresh."

He remained silent for some moments. Then he continued with a shivering voice, "But what I loved was her soul, what she was."

"Oh, thanks Jones. Thank you."

Then she faced me and said, "But David I wished we had a child too and I could sit and talk with them about Jones's good characteristics...about his generosity...about..."

Jones interrupted her and said," Hey, that's enough. I don't want to hear more. You are lying all the time."

"I must talk. I have also got some things to tell David."

"You must say nothing."

They were arguing severely.

"Why shouldn't I say anything?"

"No more talking."

"But I want to tell him that..."

Jones got up, took the handles of her wheelchair and said, "Now that it is like this, you must go to your room and leave us alone."

And as he took her to the other room, Liza shouted loudly, "David, come here when Jones is out. I tell you everything. Do come."

Sure Mrs. Loren. I come to you once to tell me everything.

Jones came back to the living room and said, "Women have bad characteristics which cannot be changed and one of them is that they talk too much. What about having a drink together?"

"No, thanks. Telling the truth, I came here to talk with you about something. I also really missed you but in fact I came for something."

"That's ok. Let's go to the yard to show you the beautiful flowers that I planted myself. Activities like this are very enjoyable during retirement."

We went to a green yard. All around the yard was covered with white and red rose bushes. We went and sat on a seat under the shade of a plane tree.

"Well, what's up? Is everything ok?"

"I want to tell you something and I want it to be between you and me. Do you promise?"

He narrowed his blue eyes and said," Well, I must know first..."

I interrupted him and said, "No, I just want some information about the operation which was taken place by the organization."

"The operation which was under my command, you mean?"

"No, this operation was after your leaving. You were retired in January and this operation was fulfilled two months ago in May."

"Well, how can I give you information about the operation which has been fulfilled during my retirement and I had no role in it?"

I kept silent for some moments. Jones was waiting for me to answer. The awesome scenes of that operation were passing by my eyes.

"David, are you crying!?"

I came back to myself and was astonished with the tears that filled my eyes. I cleared my face and said," Let me tell you the whole story. A secret operation was performed in May. We were fifty forces who were appointed for a mission under the command of Cliff..."

He interrupted me and asked loudly, "Daggles Cliff!?"

"Yes."

"You are surely making a mistake. Daggles got retired along with me. Of course it was an unexpected retirement. Our retirements were confirmed together. Didn't you know about that?"

"I didn't know about that and I didn't hear anything about it. As you said it was an unexpected retirement...like yours."

"I had my own reasons."

"He also definitely had his own reasons."

Jones looked around as if someone was spying him. He looked at me again and said, "Well, I am curious to know more...tell me more about what happened."

I continued, "We were supposed to go to a region in an African country in order to rescue some doctors, dispatched by the United Nations, whom were taken captive by the rebels. They said nothing about either the name of the country or the region. They just said that everything was secret."

"Well, a secret operation is usually done like this. It isn't unusual. You know better than me. But the presence of Daggles in the operation is weird as well as what hurt you in this operation."

I remained silent again. I bit my lips. My throat was clogged by sadness and I was on the verge of tears.

"Tell me David...tell me."

I described each and every moment of the event which was passing by my eyes. I tried to control my tears.

"We got off a helicopter in a wild land. We walked about one hour until we reached a village which was located in the middle of some woody hills. We had camouflaged and were waiting for Daggles who was reporting the procedure of the operation, to receive the order of attack. Daggles commanded us to be ready for the attack and alerted us to start the operation within five minutes. We kept the region under surveillance by camera. We were supposed to attack to a building that Daggles showed it to me before and I could easily see it by my camera in order to rescue the doctors. Some armed people were on the roof of that building but attacking the building wasn't a difficult job. We were divided into two groups. One group was under the command of Daggles and the other one was under my command to enter the village through another direction.

While we were in camouflage, we were intruding through the trees when I noticed some SUVs stuffed with local armed forces were approaching. They were shooting ruthlessly. They were shooting, by machine gun or RPG, everything and everyone on their way, women, children and so on. Some moments later we were commanded to stop the operation. The village was set into fire during the short past moments. They gathered many women and children in the middle of the village. Daggles ordered me to return to the region in which we were separated and stayed there so as that we all together could withdraw. But something didn't let me do that. There was a village which was burning in fire and there were also women and children whom were slaughtered. I called Daggles on the radio and said, "From weasel to otter." We must attack. They are slaying everyone. We are here to rescue the doctors. We are also duty bound to rescue the oppressed people. If we don't attack these guys, they kill everyone. They not only kill the doctors dispatched by the organization but also all people in here. Look at them, commander. Look well.

He laughed and said, "You are an experienced commando. We don't do anything without my command."

I said, "Commander Cliff, but we can rescue the rest of people within the village. Look, they have gathered all women and children in the middle of the village. I have no doubt they wouldn't likewise have a good behavior with them. We should attack. What about the organization's doctors? Most of those people are women and children. They can't defend themselves."

He said, "Just right now, they announced the doctors had been conveyed to another place from this village. We have nothing to do more in here. The operation has been canceled. No more arguing with me. I will withdraw the forces. You must also take the forces back within ten minutes. Do you understand?"

My forces were looking at me and waiting for me to give the command of withdrawal but I didn't say anything. I took the camera and was watching the whole events which were taking place moment by moment. I was keeping the village under surveillance from a high place. The rebels gathered women, children and some young boys in the middle of the village. They killed every old man with no hesitation. Then they kept the women and children away. A tall thin Black who seemed to be their commander along with a blond medium White who wasn't definitely an African guy was both approaching them. I couldn't hear them well from that distance but I guessed the Black translated the White's talks for people.

Then the black man separated one of the young boys and aimed his Colt at his head as if he wanted to threaten them to prize information out of them but nobody talked. He shot the boy's jaw. His jaw was broken and separated from his face, hanging from one side. His jaw was swinging and the boy himself was tottering. He was shocked. He didn't know what to do. Then some of the rebels fusilladed him.

Daggles said on the radio, "From weasel to otter. Where are you? Report your situation."

I answered, "We are not in a good situation now. The operation might be leaked. We will act some minutes later. I see some people come towards us. I must be sure about the security of our action in returning. The operation might be leaked by each wrong action."

My group members were ready for my command without being evident of what was taking place in there as they were hiding among those massy trees. I ordered them to go fifty meters back and wait my order for withdrawal. I kept the village under my surveillance again through the camera. The black man went and separated another boy from the others. Nobody said anything. Nobody complained. The people of the village were like hens and roosters that couldn't do anything and the slaughterer chose and separated anyone as he wished and cut off their necks.

There was a little boy about ten or twelve. Again the black man put his gun on his head and looked at the people. He said something and then waited for the answer. But it seemed nobody answered. Then he pushed him away. He went towards the other people and pulled out a woman who had a projected stomach. He ripped the woman's dress. The woman was shaking. He stripped her entirely. The black man faced the people and said something again but didn't get any answer. He took out a knife out of his waist and kept under the woman's stomach. He was still looking at people and expecting an answer. But nobody talked. He was shouting and was so angry that I could easily see the swollen vessels of his neck. All of a sudden he pierced the knife beneath her stomach and stretched it from one side to the other. Water and blood splashed out of her stomach and then the fetus fell out of her stomach.

The woman screamed and fell on the ground while she was shocked and listless with an open mouth. The black man who couldn't pump them for an answer became furious and shouted restlessly. The White man was busy with smoking and was watching the events as if it was a performance.

The Black man pointed at the woman and the fetus on the ground and said something. Nobody talked again. The fetus was moving on the ground. It was alive as if it was breathing. The black man went towards the fetus and kicked it away like a football. The umbilical cord was still connecting mother to her fetus. Then he shot her down.

I couldn't stand anymore. Nothing was important for me anymore...anything. It was just me and my gun camera. I aimed with no hesitation. I shot directly the black man's bald head. The skull of his head was ripped and thrown into the air. The blood was splashed onto the white man's face. All of a sudden all rebels fell into hustle and bustle. They shot around out of fear with no aim and ran towards the cars. They got into them and escaped as quickly as they could.

I looked at Jones and said, "Just by my one bullet, Jones. Just my one bullet frightened them in a way that made them escape. But why shouldn't we attack to prevent all those events and the assassination of people. At that time I lost my belief to God. God died. Everything died. It has been a long time that I haven't been able to forget those scenes of assassination. I am afflicted with nightmare each and every night. Sara has got worried for me. She is not also in good mood when she sees I behave like this. I am not an inexperienced commando. My trainings were under your surveillance. I was in many wars and conflicts. Whenever the situation required help, we killed to rescue others and we should also have killed this time to prevent the assassination of the defenseless people. We could defend but we didn't. Although the operation was for rescuing the doctors but it was also a philanthropic duty to defend the people of the village. But we didn't. Why Jones? The command for withdrawal was suspicious. It was suspicious that Daggles said the doctors were transferred to another place. I can swear that each word uttered out of his mouth had the dirty smell of lying. We have taken part in many operations, Jones. Many times, many missions weren't a part of our operation, but when we recognized it was necessary, we defended people...because we are the soldiers of the United Nations. The soldiers of all nations..."

Jones's head was down and was pressing both sides of his head by his palms during my description of those events. When I finished with my talks, he raised his fist and beat it harshly on the table in a way that the two glasses on the table were jumped out into the air and fell on the ground. Then he pointed at me with his forefinger. The blood vessels on the white part of his eyes could easily be seen. He said, "David, listen carefully... I am going to give you an advice! I don't know if you came from those dirty guys to examine me or all you said really happened. I don't know why you damn guy are here. Just I ask you to keep aloof from me. Go to hell. Did you get?"

Without getting any answer from me, he left me quickly. I was petrified for some minutes. Then I got up and set off for home. I was more astonished and absentminded than before. I was thoroughly hopeful that he could guide me what to do. I expected him to tell me something to make me calm but his reaction made me more curious than before. I didn't know what to do. I didn't know why he behaved like this. All events which were taking place were disturbing me.

After visiting Jones, first I decided not to chase anything anymore but I couldn't. Next day I called him at his home. Liza picked up the phone.

I said, "Hello Mrs. Loren. I am David."

I expected her to talk to me in a warm and intimate manner as she spoke to me the day before but she said, "Please David, Don't call again." And then she cut off the phone.

But I became more decisive to gain more information. I didn't see Daggles Cliff no more after the operation. The other soldiers in the operation were also completely ignorant about the events which took place. They just knew there was an operation and then it was cancelled. I was deadly alone but this loneliness couldn't impede me not to follow my aims. After a while, my researches went to nowhere for finding the main reason which caused the cancelation of the operation T2 and visiting Jones also made me more turbulent.

Despite of getting more information, everything became more complicated the more I went forward.

By entering the security system of the intelligence service, I realized that there was no record of such an operation within the system. All forces participating in the operation had been given a two-days off permission so there was no doubt that they played with us but the issue that who played with us and why, was something that I couldn't make a head or tail of it.

So I kept on chasing to find Daggles Cliff's house and I found him. While he was shopping in the shopping center, I pretended I saw him accidentally. I invited him for a drink. I poisoned him and by pretending that I wanted to take him to the hospital, I took him to that desolate cellar and...

Wait! By the way how do you feel now? What are you thinking about? Tell me the truth. Don't you say to yourself that I wish that cutting machine had been in my hand to chop him? No? Maybe yes and maybe no. but I don't think that you have the same idea about me as you had in the beginning of the story.

Some days after killing Daggles, I opened the door of my

house with my key and entered it. It wasn't locked so Sara surely came back home from the climbing tour. I entered the house and tried to forget the sadness that seized my whole soul.

It seemed Sara got home before me and slept. As soon as I opened the door she got up and came towards me while she was sleepy. She kissed me but she was too tired to do anything else. She nearly passed out in my huge. I hugged her and put her in her bed. Then she opened her eyes with difficulty and said, "PHYOO, What a bad odor is coming from you. Where were you?"

I looked at her with astonishment. I smelled myself and said I have no bad smelling.

Sara closed her eyes and said, "Yes, you have a bad smell. Do take a shower."

Despite of this issue that my smelling ability is many times more than a usual man and I knew that my body had no bad smell, I went to take a shower.

When I was in the shower, there was a strange smell from the living room. I opened the bath door slowly and looked outside. I didn't see anyone but that strange smell wasn't Sara's. It was an unknown smell. I took a quick shower and got out. Now there were two unknown smells. I went into the bedroom and had a look inside. Sara was asleep and pulled the sheet over her head.

Two hours were still left to my sleeping time. I turned off the house lights and lounged on the sofa in front of the TV. Some days passed by and I couldn't still forget Jones's talks as well as his furious face. His talks were all Greek to me and this issue bothered me more.

"I don't know if you came from those dirty guys to examine me? I don't know if you came from those dirty guys to examine me?"

Oh damn! Which dirty guys you mean? Why didn't you stay to talk more?

In all those days in which I became just like lunatics, sleepless and ill-humored, I asked myself, "Did I kill a man"?

Thinking profoundly, what does the word, "man" mean? Why do we name every creature a man because they have the same physical appearance as others? Oh, man, what a simple and complicated word.

My eyes couldn't stand being open anymore in front of the TV. I slept about one hour

and then I felt Sara was awake but I didn't get up. I liked to pretend to be asleep. I liked her to come to me after her rest and to wake me up by her warm kisses and ...

But I didn't know why I could still smell both strange odors. One of those smells was familiar but it wasn't the usual odor that I always smelled in my house. It was a smell which was familiar to me outside. I thought I was surely making a mistake. I was sure that Sara would come to me within some moments and my whole soul was ready to hug her but she didn't come. I felt she was going towards the kitchen. A kind of fear threw shiver to my body.

Once again, Jones's statement came to my mind, "I don't know if you came from those dirty guys to examine me? " I jumped out of my seat all of a sudden and a bullet was shot at the TV as I wanted to go towards the bedroom. Then I was petrified in darkness by seeing a man standing in front of me, aiming a Colt at me. I kept my breath inside and opened my arms. Times and times people pulled a gun on me and I got their guns within some seconds and fixed them up. I looked at the Colt. It was equipped with muffler. I was afraid for a moment that he might have killed Sara. And once again, Jones's statement came to my mind, "I don't know if you came from those dirty guys to examine me? " All those thought came into my mind for some seconds. Just the moon's light lit the darkness of the house so I couldn't see his face. But the way he was holding the Colt indicated that he was a full-scale professional. He also entered the house in a way that I didn't notice and this issue confirmed his professionalism.

"Who are you? What do you want damn guy?"

"Turn back and knee. Put your hands on the back of your head. With a smallest move..."

I interrupted him and said, "Major Jones."

"Shut your mouth and do as I said. Did you get or not?"

I turned back and kneed. I put my hands on the back of my head. One meter distance between us was enough for me to get his Colt somehow. But Jones was above me in ranking and too professional so he never came nearer. He definitely knew blocking techniques for my attacking movements.

By keeping the same distance from me, he turned round the room and stood in front of me. Then he sat on the table.

I asked, "Where is Sara?"

"She is fine. She is asleep."

As he was sitting, he put the Colt on his lap and scratched his chin as if he was under pressure how to start an argument.

He said, "Well, David, tell me who appointed you to come to me?"

I said, "You are making a mistake. I am not an emissary."

"Don't deny David. Tell the truth. I know you well."

"Jones I don't know what you are talking about. I came to you to talk about T2 operation and you behaved me like that. Well, it wasn't too bad. At least I found that you were also involved in that operation."

"Stop nonsense David! I never involved in that operation. I didn't even know there was such an operation."

"Well, it isn't wired if you deny that. It was a disgusting operation. In such situations, people don't usually accept the responsibility of an operation and claim someone else has been responsible for the events."

"Well, so you want to evade. Get up and come to the bedroom."

He moved backwards towards the bedroom while facing me. He entered the bedroom. He was aiming his Colt at me. Then he aimed it at Sara whose body was hidden completely under the sheet.

He said in low voice, "Tell me David. Tell me. I have nothing more to lose."

Jones was exactly aiming Sara's head.

"I have nothing to say. I don't know what you are after."

I uttered my last statement aloud in order to wake up Sara but she didn't have the smallest movement and it made me more worried that he might have throttled her.

Jones asked, "I ask once more. Who appointed you to come to me?"

I smiled and said, "You are making a mistake. Nobody appointed me."

Suddenly he shot at Sara on the head. Blood soaked the sheet in a round shape and the sound of the breaking of skull shocked me. My heart was getting out of my chest. I couldn't believe my eyes. It was like a nightmare but it wasn't a nightmare.

Times and times I was witness of the scene of breaking of skulls in various operations. In an operation in Somalia, we were a twelve-member team that was surrounded by the rebels. We were all kneeing and putting our hands behind our heads.

The head of the rebels who was a young thin man was walking in front of us. He was so slim that I swear I was able shoot him away just by one fist blow. He was holding a bottle of wine in one hand and drank it. He also had a Colt in his other hand. One of the scenes that always make me laugh is the scene of the guys who are physically thin and weak but they feel like a Hercules by holding a Colt in their hands while drinking wine. It was a solitude village in the north of Somalia but stupid guys like this one can also be found within the big cities too; guys who probably die before their hair turns white.

He talked with his friends. They made a group of four people and stood in a line direction like a fire squad.

They pulled out one of us and took him in front of a wall with a distance about ten meters from it. The first one kept up his Colt, aimed and shot. The bullet cut my friend's ear and stuck it on the wall.

The second one pulled the Colt and shot the upper part of his leg. The third one who was the young thin man shot. The bullet stroke the wall and his friends burst into laughter. He tried to avoid laughing by shouting but the more he shouted, the more they laughed. He went towards my friend and took him by the collar. He took out a hatchet out of his pants stock and beat it on his head again and again and again.

But at that moment, by seeing Sara's disintegrated head in front of my eyes, I couldn't make a right decision. I leaped over towards his stomach. My head got hot. The only thing that I was thinking about was how I could squash his head. The Colt was thrown under the bed and we were in conflict. We stroke each other in any possible way and by each object which was reachable. As we were entangled, I stretched my arm, took a perfume and smashed it on his face. He took the brush and beat it on my head. I took the hair-dryer and smashed it on his head. He took the hair-dryer wire and twisted it around my neck. I was throttling. I kicked his stomach. He got stuck to the wall. I leaped over for the Colt. He tripped me over. I fell on the ground but the Colt was in my hand. I kept it in front of his face. He also raised a vase above his head to smash it onto my head.

We both were petrified. The smallest move by him could be lead to his head disintegration. He knew about my speed in my reaction as well as my attention in shooting. In that situation, I was also able to aim the mole of his cheek if I wanted.

I said, "Now it is your turn to answer my question, Major."

I continued with shouting, "Well your hands are tired. Put the vase aside and answer me, you bastard piece of nothing."

He slowly brought down his hands and put the vase on the table.

He asked, "What must I say?"

There was a lump in my throat and I wanted to cry. I smiled and said, "I don't think it is a good time for evading. You know, in fact you are dead right now. Tell me who ordered the command of withdrawal?"

He asked, "Is this just the only thing you are really after it?"

I was shivering. The Colt was shivering in my hand.

I said, "It is the only thing I am after it. Now first you talk and then you die or you just die. Of course it makes no difference for me. I will find the truth sooner or later."

He said, "Look at the bed. Keep calm. She isn't Sara."

I looked at the bed. First I thought he was tricking to attack me again. But he wasn't in a situation that he could do something. The bullet pierced the sheet and the blood ran. The sound of the breaking of the skull wasn't also an unfamiliar sound that made me think I might make a mistake. How couldn't she be Sara? But my smelling ability confirmed Jones's words. Sara's smell was coming from a further distance.

He said, "Sara hasn't died. Check it. She isn't Sara. I stand opposite the wall to assure you it isn't a trick."

He faced the wall. I pulled aside the sheet. It was a woman with red hair who was throttled with a rope around her neck. Jones's shot also disintegrated her skull. I aimed the Colt at Jones again and said, "Turn back."

He turned back and said, "Sara is in the kitchen, alive and kicking."

I walked backwards while facing Jones. Sara was on the corner of the kitchen with closed hands and feet. She tried to talk but she was just mourning. I went towards her and opened her hands and feet. I could smell Jones's odor which was getting closer. I aimed the Colt rapidly at the door of the kitchen. He appeared within the framework of the door.

He said, "David, You were awesome the recent last days and especially tonight. I can't believe at all that a commando like you behave so foolishly and inconsiderately. What you did was a catastrophe. Get up. We are out of time. We must all leave less than five minutes. Hurry up. Take everything that you need. We never come back again."

I asked," Why must we escape? Why should I trust you?"

You see that Sara is alive and someone else is on bed with disintegrated skull. Now it depends on you if you want to trust me or not.

I had no choice. I had to trust him. He would kill me if he really wanted to kill me. Even when I attacked him, he could shoot me but he didn't. We put everything in a bag less than five minutes. Sara was vomiting in the toilet. I was worried for her. Jones called me from the kitchen. He was holding a hatchet in his hand.

He said, "Put your hand on the table."

I asked, "Why?"

He said, "I must cut the head of the little finger of your left hand."

I asked, "The head of the little finger of my left hand? For what?"

He said, “Because it is equipped with detector. If you don’t remove it, we will be traced.”

I stood up and was thinking about what he said. The sound of vomiting also disturbed the trend of my mind.

He said, “Hurry damn guy. We have no time. Hurry, I don’t want to kill you.”

I said, “I shit your brain if you make a mistake.”

He fastened a band tightly at the bottom of my finger to prevent bleeding. I put my palm on the ground and opened my fingers. Jones cut it off skillfully. There was bleeding, burning paining and shouting.

After five minutes, we got into Jones’s car and we were riding in a highway out of the city to an unknown destination.

Sara and I were sitting at the back seats. Sara who had a tiresome and frightening day, put her head on my laps and closed her eyes. Once in a while, she got up and vomited and then put her head on my laps. Something damn was wrong with her because she held a handkerchief on her nose as if she was irritated by smell. Her body was shivering. I knew she wasn’t asleep and just tried to sleep but she couldn’t.

I drew back her hair with my hand and tried to calm her by stroking her face. It was good that my finger was numb at that time but I knew that it wouldn't take a long time and the pain would start soon.

I asked," Where are we going Jones? Why did they want to kill me? How did you know about that?"

"I have nothing to say at present. Don't ask anything."

A sound was heard from the trunk of the car. I was frightened. Sara was also frightened. She raised her head from my lap and sat. We both gazed at Jones.

I asked, "Is there anyone in the trunk?"

He said, "God damn me. I am such an absent-minded fool."

He pulled over the car and got out of it. I didn't trust anything. I kept the Colt tightly in my hand and was tracing Jones with my eyes. He opened the trunk. I heard Liza's voice and then I saw Jones who hugged her.

She said, "Damn with you Jones. You don't care me at all."

Jones opened the back door and said, "Let Liza sit beside Sara. Come and sit in front."

By seeing Liza I became calmer. I felt Jones couldn't be dangerous for us anymore but in spite of this we still had to be cautious. I sat on the front seat beside Jones. Liza was looked at Sara's face and said, "Oh, don't worry my dear; everything will be all right. I promise."

Liza's words made me calmer. I looked at Sara and I felt that she wasn't worried as much as before. She couldn't forget easily what happened at home. Liza took my shoulder from behind and said, "Your wife is very beautiful. You are a lucky man."

We were riding nonstop in the car for about two hours on a highway then Jones rode the car onto a bypath. He also turned off the car's lights. We didn't have any clear sight and if we didn't have the moonlight too, we would definitely lose the bypath direction too. He stopped the car. My finger started to pain and was making me crazy. Jones noticed my pain. He brought out two tablets out of the dashboard, gave them to me and said, "Eat both together."

He took his cell phone out of his pocket and dialed a number. He said on the phone, "We are exactly where you appointed."

He cut off the phone. Who was waiting for us? With who was he coordinated? Where were we supposed to go? What was ahead of us? There were a lot of questions and worries that shook my whole soul. None of those questions might be of any significance for me if Sara wasn't with me but the presence of Sara, the only person whom I loved in this world from the bottom of my heart, in that situation made me more frightened.

We were waiting speechless for two hours in that darkness until we heard the sound of a helicopter that was approaching us. I was afraid of the police tracing. I looked at Jones. He was calm and this calmness made me more furious rather than giving me more tranquility. He didn't also say anything. The helicopter turned on its light and directed it on us. Jones got out of the car and signed the helicopter by moving his hands in an X shape.

A man with an average height and a bulgy stomach got off the helicopter with difficulty and came towards us. He was limping on his left leg while he was walking. Jones went towards him and they hugged each other. None of them, the man as well as the helicopter was a military one. Nothing was more itching than the hours ahead which I had no idea about.

I turned back and looked at Sara. I smiled and then got out of the car. I went towards them. They were reciprocating good words and feelings when they saw me.

Jones said, "This is my friend...the one you were after him. Then he continued, David, this is Tony Bear. We called him before, Polar Bear." Then they laughed loudly together.

Tony and I shook hands and then Tony said, "Hey ape, how do you do? If you know what Jones and I did for you, you would really appreciate us."

Tony and Jones laughed. Jones went towards the car and opened the door. I heard Liza who said loudly with joking and laughing, "Jones, if I knew I was supposed to see Tony, I would never come with you."

Tony who heard Liza's voice, went towards the car and said aloud, "Oh my Goodness! Beautiful Liza is here too? Come on Liza...come on as I missed you so much."

He got into the car with half of his body inside and Liza's laugh was heard. Some moments later, exactly like a child, he held Liza in his arms and said, "My dear, I missed you so much. Look, I brought a helicopter for you not to be tired more than this."

Sara also got out of the car and came towards the helicopter. She sat and vomited again.

I have never felt so dump, absentminded and clumsy in my life. Sara came closer and put her head on my chest. I pressed her on my chest and kissed her forehead. We all got on the helicopter. Big Tony was the pilot. I thought the seats in the helicopter couldn't be comfortable but they were as if they were made for resting and recreation.

I became way-worn out of tiredness, stress and sleeplessness. Sara was either the same. She put her head on my shoulder and closed her eyes. As always, she held my hands with both her hands, sticking them on her chest. Moments later my hands set free out of her hands and I got that she fell into sleep. She could sleep in spite of all those anxiety and worriment and it made me both astonished and happy. After about an hour of flying, we reached a region which was like a garrison. It was a place with a shooting area at one side and military equipment on the other side. We landed. Sara was still sleeping. I slapped her softly many times to wake her up.

I said, "We reached."

"Where is it?" She asked while she was dizzy and sleepy.

I shrugged and said, "I don't know."

Tony Bear said, "Here is my house. Don't worry. Everything is ok in here."

We went towards the building. I estimated the height of the building in my mind. We entered. I was reviewing everything in my mind, the entrance door, stairs, windows, the height of walls, the building floor, walls and everything within the house.

Tony Bear who got out of breath by walking, showed a room to me and said, "This is for you and Sara. There are also toilet and bath in there. The fridge is also full. But now that you feel sleepy like an ape; it is better to sleep damn until tomorrow morning."

Jones who was pushing Liza's wheelchair, entered the house. My voice echoed within the whole house by shouting loudly, "Sleep damn? I don't understand. I don't understand at all. What are we doing here? Who are you? Why should we be here? Who were the people who wanted to kill me? How did you know that I was supposed to be killed that made you help me? Where is this place? I haven't come such a long way to here that you tell me to sleep damn. Do you think I can close my eyes even for a moment?"

Tony Bear said, "Sleep damn until tomorrow morning."

I said," I can't. I must know where and why just right now?"

He said, "You stinky ape, don't talk like a creditor. We toiled a lot to reuse you and your wife."

I said, "Who told you to toil for rescuing us?"

Jones, "I said buddy. The organization kept you under surveillance and the intelligence service which was looking for Daggles Cliff reached you in the wake of their researching. They got that you had a role in his absence. After you left me, I called Tony and asked him to keep you under surveillance.

I asked, "The absence of Daggles Cliff!? Tony, organization, I don't understand at all. Is he lost? Is Tony also the organization's member?

He said, "Not now but he has some people within the organization who work for him and report us any information he wants to gain..."

I interrupted him and asked, "Has he some people in the organization!? What is his job that he has some people in the organization? What is the relevance between the absence of Daggles and me?"

He continued without paying any attention to my questions, "We became aware that they appointed a professional group for killing you. When we found this, we started to do something for you and Sara and if we had been late for taking an action you both would have been killed so far."

I became more confounded and deuced.

I said, "Did the organization appoint a professional assassination team for killing me? Oh, my God! What a ridiculous story! Hahaha...look, I am laughing. Why must they do that?

Tony Bear puffed his cheeks and said, "It is your fault, Jones. You should have let them shoot him on the head then he could believe what you said.

Then he faced me and said, "So do you want to deny that you killed Daggles?"

I asked," Is he killed? Why?"

Tony Bear smiled, faced Jones and said, "This ape wants to act for us. You said that he was a professional commando but you didn't say he was a good actor too."

Jones took out his cell phone out of his pocket and said, "Turn on your Bluetooth."

I turned it on. He sent a film to me. Sara was sitting on the sofa and eating her finger's nail. She used to do that whenever she was agitated. I opened the film. It was the scene of butchering Daggles. It was unbelievable but it was true. A film with excellent quality and a clear voice. I couldn't believe they took a film from me but it was true. The film was also taken from a close distance. With regard to the angles as well as the movements of the camera, I found that the film was taken by a mouse camera.

I wanted to say something when Tony Bear said, "Just shut up now. We are all tired. It is better to sleep. I know you have a lot of questions but ask them for tomorrow."

I stood and gazed at him. He clenched one fist, smashed it on his palm and said, "Hey ape, for God's sake, just shut up and sleep until tomorrow."

I looked at Sara. She seemed more agitated than me. We went towards the bedroom. I opened the door and entered it. Sara lay on bed without taking off his cloth. But I knew that her female curiosity made her have more questions than me and like Tony Bear, I wasn't in good mood for answering.

I was examining everything in the room, windows, height of wall, whatsoever within the fridge, bath, toilet, under the bed, plugs and so on when Sara asked, "Did you kill anyone, David?"

I hesitated in answering and said, "No."

She asked, "Can I see that film?"

I asked, "Which film?"

She said, "The film that Jones sent to your Bluetooth."

I said, "No."

She asked, "Why not? Why shouldn't I know anything? It has been about a couple of hours that I have been speechless and didn't ask anything. Can I ask a question now?"

I said," No, not now. Please sleep damn and don't say anything."

She lay on bed while she was going to burst into tears. She was tired and shivering. I was tired as much as she was but I couldn't close my eyes. It became a confusing play. Me, Daggles, filming, organization, hiring assassinator for me, Big Tony, Jones, Liza and the place that I didn't know where it was. I had no choice but to wait.

I lay on bed. I was looking at the ceiling and reviewed all events which took place. I could find no connection point among them. Now they knew that I killed Daggles cliff. Well! Daggles was a retired man so it was the police which had to trace me not the organization, especially by hiring an assassination team.

Whenever I place in a difficult situation, I remember my mother and I also remembered her in that situation. When I remember her, I feel that I put my head on her laps and she strokes my head. One day after finishing playing football, I was going home. The sun was going to set down. My mother used to tell me, "You must be at home before sunset. A good boy must be with his family at night."

When I was coming back home, I saw that a car fell into a small hole from one side. Its driver was a young woman. I passed by it. She looked at me. I felt she needed help. I asked, "Can I help you?"

She smiled, shrugged and said, "I don't think. The car has fallen into a hole. You can't do anything alone."

I said, "Let me try."

She asked, "How?"

I said, "You sit at the steering wheel and press the accelerator. I push the car from behind."

She said, "No, you can't do it alone."

I said, "This street is very empty at this time and you might not find someone else to help you but I can do it now. Let me try."

The woman nodded and said, "Ok, we will try."

She pulled back her entire blond hair and tied it at the back. She sat at the steering wheel, started the car and pressed the accelerator. The wheel was turning without going forward. I pushed it for some seconds but it didn't move. She got out of the car and said, "I told you that we can't do it."

I looked at her and said, "Something stroke my mind. Please wait." I found a stone and put it in the empty place between the wheel and the hole's wall. Then I stood aside and said, "I think it will come out now even without pushing."

The woman shrugged, got into the car and pressed the accelerator again. The car came out of the hole easily. The woman smiled and said, "You are very clever."

I said, "Thanks mam. "

She said, "Let me ride you home."

I thanked her and kept on my way to home. I didn't notice it was getting dark and when I came into myself, I couldn't believe it had got dark. I didn't realize how much time I was busy with the car. I ran towards the house. I was sure my mother got worried for me. I ran the entire street to reach the head of the alley. When I turned into the alley, I lost my balance and I had to keep myself stable by holding some boxes which were put in front of the shop which was placed on the corner. They moved and some of them fell on the ground. Before the shopkeeper came out, I had run a couple of meters in the darkness. I heard Aboutaleb, the owner of the shop shout and say something. I didn't know if he was complaining or cursing at me. When I reached home, I knocked on the door incessantly. My mother opened the door. My eyes were filled with tears. I greeted. She didn't answer. I found that she was angry. I entered the house. I thought about the young woman and Aboutaleb – one made me happy and the other one made me sad. I tried to talk to my mother. I asked, "Hasn't daddy come back home?"

She didn't answer.

I said, "Today my teacher asked me some questions at the whiteboard. I answered all of them and got a good mark."

She didn't answer.

I asked, "Mummy, do you sing a song for me?"

She didn't answer. She was preparing the food in the kitchen.

I said, "I am sorry mummy."

She didn't answer again. I burst into tears and said, "I am sorry mummy. Swear to God. I don't repeat it again. I promise."

He looked at me and said, "Didn't I tell you to be at home before darkness?"

I said, "I always come back soon; you know it."

She said, "Ok, now tell me...why were you late this time?"

I told her what happened. She smiled and said, "Ok, I make up with you for your good deed but never be late again."

She hugged me and I put my head on her chest. She put her arms around me. I raised my head and said, "Kiss me, kiss, kiss, kiss."

She bent his neck and kissed me. She cleared my tears. My father was at night shift. We ate dinner. She used to tell me a story at night. She sat on the bed and I put my head on her laps. She used to keep on telling stories until I fell asleep. That night she told me some stories like the other nights but it took a long time and I couldn't sleep. My eyes were open.

She looked at me and asked, "What are you thinking about, David?"

I said, "Nothing."

She said, "But mothers find when their children think about something. You are thinking about something. Do you like us to talk about it?"

I said, "I am afraid."

She asked, "Of me?"

I said, "No, I am afraid that if I tell you what happened, you get upset and don't like me anymore."

She said, "Mothers can't break down with their children forever. David, now tell me what happened?"

I told her what happened on my way when I was coming back home.

She looked at me and said, "Well, this accident happened but we must pay for the damage."

And it was the very thing which I was afraid of. Going to that shop and encountering Aboutaleb. He was a Muslim and what I had in my mind about Muslims in that time was that they were wild people. We saw in television that there had always been war in Muslim countries, in Afghanistan, Iran and Iraq.

My mother continued, "Always try not to make a mistake and if you made a mistake try to compensate."

I said, "But Aboutaleb is a Muslim and he might..." And I didn't finish my statement.

My mother said, "Well, no problem if he is a Muslim. Who said Muslims are bad people? We are Christian and they are Muslim. Aboutaleb likes the Christ and the Profit Maryam so much. Real Muslims are good people; better than what you think. Tomorrow we go together to him. We apologize and we pay for the damage.

All night, going to Aboutaleb's shop passed by my eyes in various scenes until I slept. When we woke up in the morning, my mother put on her clothes and we went together to Aboutaleb's shop. Aboutaleb wasn't in the shop and the cashier said that he was in the storeroom.

My mother and I went towards the storeroom which was in the end of the shop. My mother called him, "Mr. Aboutaleb... Mr. Aboutaleb."

His harsh voice shook my body and said, "Yes mam. I am coming."

Moments later, he came out from behind the packages within the storeroom. When he saw my mother and I, he smiled and said, "I am at your service. What is the problem? Is something wrong with what you bought from the shop? Don't worry. I change it for you."

My mother said, "No...no, I have never had any problem with your goods and I have always been satisfied with them. We came to apologize."

My head was down and my mother continued, "My son was in a hurry when was coming back home last night. He hit the boxes in front of your shop but he was afraid and couldn't apologize. Now we have come to apologize and pay for the damage if there is one.

My head was still down but I felt he was looking at me. I looked up and his smile made me calm.

He said, "Bravo my good boy. Bravo that you came back and apologized. Well, you didn't intentionally throw the boxes, did you?"

I said, "No...anywise. I was just in a hurry. That was all."

He stretched his arm towards me and said, "So let's shake hands because there is no problem between us. You didn't do it intentionally and I have no complain." I also stretched my arm and put my hand in his big warm hand. We shook hands and then he said, "We are friends forever."

My mother said, "You are a great and kind man. How much did we damage? I will pay all."

Aboutaleb stroked his white beard and said, "There was no damage. Some boxes fell down and I put them away. Nothing more happened and I am very happy for this accident which led to our more acquaintance. I know your husband. He is an honorable man. I know that he has to work at night and sometimes in the other cities. Please give my regards to him."

My mother and I looked at each other and laughed. After that accident, whenever I heard the word, "Muslim", I remembered the kind face of Aboutaleb.

I said, "If you don't mind my saying, I want to tell you something."

My mother looked at me with astonishment. So did Aboutaleb.

He said, "Tell me. I hope it wouldn't be like that."

I pointed to a corner with my finger and said, "There is a mouse hole in there."

Aboutaleb smiled and said, "Naughty boy! Do you want to say that you put them in there? But there is no mouse in here."

My mother who was very worried and embarrassed that lest I might say something bad, looked up and said, "Trust my boy. David's smelling ability is too strong."

Aboutaleb looked at my mother with an open mouth and turned back and gazed at the corner which I pointed to.

He narrowed his eyes and went towards the corner. He pulled away the boxes and said, "Oh, my God."

We left the shop. There were some recently borne mice in there whose eyes were closed and couldn't move at all.

Aboutaleb looked at me and then my mother, smiled and said, "It's unbelievable."

I put my head on mother's lap that night and she stroked my head. I was happy that she was beside me in absence of my father. I was happy that she helped me to get rid of my thoughts concerning Aboutaleb and its shop. I was so happy those days and now in Tony bear's house, I was lying on bed beside Sara and I felt my mother's empty place. At that moment I felt I needed my mother to put my head on her lap and tell her that I had done something bad. But was killing Daggles really a misdeed? The issue of Daggles wasn't like the issue of Aboutaleb and some boxes. The issue of Daggles was the issue of a man's life. Oh my God, I am really fed up with the word, "man". I am really fed up with the issue that I must use the word, "man" for any human being with arms and legs and the ability of talking. Was Daggles Cliff really a man? What do you think? Was Daggles a man? Is someone who is able to help others to prevent their death but he evades it, a man? Ah...man. What a simple and complicated word! By the way what do you think about me now? Are you still thinking I am a dirty guy?

Episode Two

I woke up by hearing the barrage sound of a machine gun and jumped out of my bed. Sara got up too and sat on the bed.

I shouted, "Lie down Sara."

She didn't know what to do. The sound was near but it wasn't from inside the building. I looked around. I looked at the door, ceiling and the kitchen. I crept towards the window. I looked out through the window from one side behind the curtain. I saw Tony and Jones who were shooting an aim board in front of the building at the shooting area.

"Shit on your shooting. It was a disaster."

I took a deep breath. I wanted to open the window and load them with curses.

"Hey you, Tony Bear, you are always boosting of your shooting. Now we see how you shoot."

I also heard Liza's voice but I couldn't see her. Tony took the machine gun from Jones. He loaded the gun and pointed at the aim board with one hand. He shot. Although it was a long distance from where I was but I could see the dust raised by the bullets shot at the boards which were arranged in a line with a given distance.

"Well, beautiful Liza, what do you think?"

"I think Polar Bear is the most professional shooter of the word...hahaha."

I turned back and looked at Sara. She was sitting while she was astonished and pale. She was also shivering. I went towards her and put her head on my chest. She didn't put her arms around my wait as she usually did it before. We didn't have anything to say. My finger was suffering from a sharp pain.

My cell phone rang. I scared. Who could it be? I looked at the number. It was unknown. I scared more. I went towards the window to tell Jones. He was holding his cell phone on his ear and was looking at our window. When he saw us he cut the phone. My cell phone's ring was cut too. With the gesture of his finger he told me to join them. A thought stoke my mind. I ran while I was going out of the building towards them.

Hey Jones, "My cell phone has been on from last night."

Tony said, "Well, what is wrong with it? So what?"

"Well, those guys can easily trace us through it."

"No ape. Before leaving your house, Jones changed your SIM card. You are such an idiot who things like this never strike your mind. If we had been in the hope of your measures, we would have been betrayed so far. You dumb ace."

I took a deep breath. Tony's cell phone rang. He looked at the number and asked us to be silent by putting his finger on his nose.

"Hey buddy! Long time no see."

"…"

"Well, what kind of mission is it?"

"…"

"Well, send the image now. I will check it on the laptop."

He came towards the table which was near Jones and I. Liza was also sitting under her sunshade. He opened the laptop. Some seconds later, the picture of Sara, Liza, Jones and I appeared on the screen.

"The pictures have been received. Now what is the mission?"

"…"

"I am inclined to perform it but you became very stingy nowadays."

"…"

"Really? That is ok. Now that it is like it, I will finish it today."

"..."

"Don't worry buddy. You are hiring Tony Bear to do the job. You can order gravestone for all of them from now."

"..."

"Oh, so without grave? That is ok."

I looked at Jones and moments later, Tony cut the phone.

Tony said, "Well Jones, my guess was right."

I asked, "Which guess?"

Tony said, "My guess about the issue that they call me and give me the mission for killing you four."

"I smiled and returned towards the building. As I was going towards the building, I yelled, "Saraaaa..."

A bullet was shot near my foot. I stopped walking. Sara was watching the scene from the window. Moments later, she got out of the building while she was running. While she was running, she screamed, "What do you want from us?"

Tony was still aiming the machine gun at us. I was furious as I was looking directly in Tony's eyes. Sara was hiding behind me. Jones raised his hand and stood between Tony and me. He said, "Stop behaving like children."

Tony got down the head of the machine gun. Jones was standing with one hand on his waist and with another hand on his chin while stroking it. Then he went towards Tony and took his arm. They went further away. They talked and then turned back towards us.

As he was going to say something, Sara said, "Please, let us go."

"Where?"

It was Liza's voice. Sara turned towards her and said, "Everywhere except here."

Liza said, "Everywhere except here means death. Do you like you and your husband to be killed Sara?"

Everybody became speechless for a moment. We were still standing. Sara's look was full of questions. The questions like, what must we do? Why don't we go? What do you want to do? Why did all those events take place? Why are we here? And...

I broke the silence and asked, "Don't anyone want to explain what all these happenings mean? Who were those who wanted to kill me?"

Jones answered incessantly, "I told you before that the organization is after you, your wife, Liza and me."

I said, "But I think you are joking."

Tony Bear put a cigar in the corner of his mouth and held a lighter at the bottom. He was looking at an unknown point. He puffed at it two or three times and asked," Joking? Hey ape, why do you think we are joking in such a situation when you put all our lives into danger? It is better your wife gets into the house then we can talk better."

I said, "Sara, please come back. I want to make it clear what is happening."

"I want to be beside you."

"Not now...please."

She pressed his lips and drew back her hair. She returned and went towards the building.

Jones asked, "Well Tony, what must we do to get out of this plight?"

Tony said, "Well it is clear. I must kill all of you and it isn't an easy job."

I asked, "So what are you waiting for? I am here and you have a gun. Finish it. How isn't it easy?"

Jones said, "What a hell is wrong with you buddy? Let us think."

I asked, "How do we think? Why do they order Tony to kill us? Who is Tony that they order him to kill us? Why does the organization hire assassinator to kill me? What is your part in this issue that they are also after you too?"

Tony said, "It is easy. You killed Daggles Cliff."

I said, "Yes, I killed him. You have the film too. So there are enough documents for putting me on trial. Why shouldn't I be brought to trial? It is right that I have killed someone but why don't they behave me like a man? How does law usually act when someone commits a crime? Do they hire an assassinator to kill the murderer?"

Liza said, "Please, all come and sit under the sunshade."

We went towards Liza and sat on the chairs under the sunshade.

Jones said, "We know the main issue but I must explain why we are all here. David you killed a senior major of the organization. We know why you killed him. Of course this senior major was retired and the question is why did he work after retirement? In fact you were among the rare soldiers who were suspicious to the organization's activities. You were searching the truth and these searches made you encounter more truth. After you came to me and told me about the T2 operation, I had no doubt that you would embark upon doing activities which might be dangerous for you so we kept you under surveillance. To prove this claim we filmed the assassination of Daggles. After his assassination, they doubted you and we found that they schemed to kill both you and your wife."

I knuckled on the table fiercely and shouted, "Well, why didn't those damn guys listen to me? Why don't they put me on trial? Why do they want to kill me without judgment?"

Tony Bear said, "Hey ape, please shut up and listen because the T2 operation was both concerned with the organization and not concerned with the organization."

"Oh my God, why don't I get a head or rail out of it? What do you mean by not concerned with the organization? We are the organization's especial military forces so what does not concerned mean?"

Tony put out his cigar in the ashtray and continued, "Look David you are our friend. That is why we are telling you what happened. We know why you killed Daggles. Our thoughts are the same. We all are struggling for humanitarianism. The T2 operation was schemed by the military forces of the organization and as you know such an operation hasn't been recorded within the organization's programs. But it hasn't been the only operation which has been like this. There have been other operations which made us suspicious. The first one who had to get out of the organization to trace the issues was me. Of course I did it with Jones's coordination. When I got out of the organization ten years ago, I formed a special private team.

I smiled and said, "You mean a team of the mercenaries? Is it right? Those who take money to kill."

"Hey ape you can think like this but don't judge soon. The issue is more complicated than what you think and you have enough time to make fun of me as well as my business. Just right now the issue is that I have been ordered to kill you four and the reason for the order is clear because the intelligence service couldn't trace you. And when their researching goes to nowhere, they call me and you must be happy for that because you are in safe place now. Anyway I have no choice but to obey this order."

I took a deep breath and said, "Mr. Professional, Mr. Tony Bear, Mr. Bastard, Mr. Mercenary, Well, you have a gun and four of us are here. You have also no choice but to abide by the order so what are you waiting for?"

"Hey ape..."

Jones raised his hand for Tony and said, "That is enough." Then he faced me and said, "It is an easy job for him if he wants to kill us but we must be alive and let him find a way for this problem. Tony is professional in programing mission like this. But please understand that we have done big jobs to rescue you and Sara. We could be nonchalant to all those events and just right now we could have been preparing to take part in you and Sara's funeral ceremony in spite of sitting here and talk. I know that you want to find out why all those events took place but after he programs the procedure of killing us, I explain you everything. I promise. But now we are out of time. Just right today Tony must finish with this job."

The he faced Tony and said, "Well Tony, what is your program for killing us?"

Tony scratched his chin and said, "I don't know. I had done before jobs like this but this time it is a bit different. Everything must be done in its best shape and as you said we are out of time."

"What must I tell Sara until the play is over?"

Tony said, "Hey ape it is your problem. Try to calm her. I can't bear women's nagging. Just shut her up. I must finish with this job until tonight or ultimately until tomorrow morning. Otherwise I am afraid that they hire other private groups to do this job. Or they might have hired other groups so far to finish it sooner. They are afraid the T2 operation data to be leaked out. Particularly now that they think David, it means you killed four people last night and escaped."

Four people!? Me? Hey wait, Jones killed the woman but who were the three others whom I didn't see?

Jones smiled and said, "Hey buddy, did you think that they ordered just one guy to kill you just like films? No, I killed three more outside."

Liza who kept silence so far said, "Wait I have a question. Tony Bear, please don't help Jones for answering this question. Let me see, if you were killed last night when you went to rescue David and Sara, what would happen to me within the trunk?"

Tony laughed aloud and said, "God damn you Jones! Did you put beautiful Liza in the trunk? You are a fool bastard!"

"Don't laugh damn bear. I want to know what does this bastard want to tell me?"

Jones pretended he was looking around while Tony was still laughing.

"Look at me Jones and answer my question bastard."

"Yes my dear, did anybody ask me a question?"

Tony was laughing louder and louder.

"Answer my question before I strangle you."

Jones took Liza's hand, kissed it and said, "Ok my dear, I answer you but now we don't have too much time. Please, let us be serious just right now...please."

Tony didn't laugh anymore.

All kept quiet and then Jones said, "Tony I think we don't really have time."

"I know damn, I am thinking."

They became silent again. Then Tony whispered to himself but it wasn't clear what he was saying.

After some moments he said, "There is no choice. I must call this guy again."

Jones asked, "Who?"

"We must appoint the prodigy to do this."

Jones said, "I also think we must do as you said but the issue is how he can do it by having the organization's confirmation? You know better that you can't report our death without a smoking gun and take your money.

"Yes I know, but both Tony Bear and the prodigy know their jobs well."

Tony took out his cellphone and dialed a number.

"Where are you ape?"

"..."

"We are in trouble. Come as soon as possible."

He cut off the phone and told me, "It is better to talk with your wife and explain her how the situation is."

I said calmly, "How should I explain the situation for Sara?"

Liza, "Let me do it. It might be so much better."

Jones nodded and continued, "Do it Liza, well done."

Liza pushed the wheels and went towards the building.

I asked, "Well what must we do now?"

Jones said, "We are waiting for the prodigy."

Who is this prodigy?

"A prodigy."

"What can he do that you call him the prodigy."

"He can do almost everything and even if he can't do it, he would learn how to do it. That is why he is a prodigy...astute and peerless. Now let's practice shooting to ease our damn stress."

We all got up and stood in a line. Jones said, "It is good to see my buddy's art of shooting."

Tony said, "I will be happy to see something considerable from this guy to stop looking at him as a fool ape."

Jones twinkled at me and said, "Well, we have five aim boards in front of us. Each aim board has three circles. David, Shoot as soon as I finish with my words. First aim board, first circle, second aim board, second circle, third aim board, first circle. Fourth aim board third circle. Fifth aim board, the right up corner. Fourth aim board, first circle. Third aim board, third circle. Second aim board, no shooting. First aim board third circle, down part."

I performed my all nine shootings incessantly and then I looked at Tony. He was gazing at the aim boards with thorough astonishment. First he looked at Jones and then at me.

Tony said, "A bird is moving within the bushes behind the aim boards. Shoot."

I aimed promptly and shot. The bird flew away.

Tony said, "You screwed it up."

"But I shot where it was."

"Anyway your shooting was a shit. I wanted you to shoot the bird."

"I was able to do it easily but I never shoot an innocuous creature. Why must I shoot it?"

"Because I asked you."

"What a hell are you whom I must obey?"

"We assume that you rescued our lives but it isn't a reason that I do something wrong because it is in accordance with your favor."

"So you are always holding tight with your beliefs."

"If I hadn't held tight with my beliefs, I wouldn't have been here now."

"Hello to all American thugs and hooligans! I am here."

We all turned back towards the voice. Tony was elated. He went towards him and hugged him. He was a man with average stature and grizzly hair.

"Hello to my ape. You are welcome."

"Hi the prodigy", Jones said it and then shook hands with him. Then he continued, "This is David and this is the prodigy.

The prodigy smiled and said, "According to Tony Bear "the ape."

Tony said, "That is over. Sit at the table. We must finish with the job. It is about noon. We don't have too much time."

We sat at the table and Tony told the prodigy that we four people had to be killed until tonight and it had to be done somehow that it seemed completely real. The prodigy turned on his i-pad and searched for something.

Moments later he asked with astonishment, "What wrong have you done?"

Tony asked, "Why are you asking this?"

They have also hired two more teams.

"Tony was sweating and his lips were shivering. What? Aren't you making a mistake? Tell us more ape."

"From six o'clock in the morning, I have noticed a couple of unusual orders. I have been curious to know what they are. I thought it had to have definitely an important reason. But now I have received some codes that are directly pertaining to the four people you pointed out."

I was trying to find out what was happening. Three teams were hired to kill us. But why three teams? I killed someone.

That was right. But there was no reason that they hired three teams for arresting me or even killing me – and why for killing four of us? What was Sara's sin? Why did they also want to kill Jones and Liza who had no role in this play? Why don't they put me on trial? Why did they stop the operation? Who stopped the operation?

When you are entangled in a plight, you have no way out. Plight is like a quagmire, the more you struggle to get out, the more you will sink. I had to control myself. But how could I do it when I was thinking about Sara? I closed my eyes and didn't like to see or to hear anything. Tony, Jones and the prodigy were permanently talking about killing us. Escaping through Canada's or Mexico's borders but none of border options was a good recommendation for our screenplay. Screenplay?!

It was the word that the prodigy used and continued, "Moving towards Pennsylvania, New Jersey, Massachusetts or any other border around this region is a ridiculous act. Taking such a measure means revealing our plan. We must exactly think like a fugitive who wants to save his life."

He faced me and said, "David, some teams of mercenaries have been hired to kill you and your wife and you have no more time. You must escape as soon as possible. Which direction do you choose?"

I thought and said, "The Ocean, it is the fastest and nearest way for escaping."

"Well done! Listen, the mercenaries know that water is the most possible best way for escaping so I promise you they are waiting for you there."

I asked, "Well, must we find another way?"

He answered, "No, we must exactly choose this way."

Tony asked, "Hey ape, you mean we go directly to the heart of those who want to kill us?"

The prodigy nodded and answered, "Yes, we must exactly go directly to the heart of those who want to kill us because the screenplay must seem real. If it wasn't the matter of escaping, you wouldn't need to move but the matter is that you four must be killed in order to live freely for the rest of your life. Of course you must also regard the matter of expenditure. The best way for all of you who are in New York is that you go through the ocean in a hidden shape. As you and Jones are both professional commandoes, they know that you will manage to do this even by a small boat to reach somewhere."

"God damn you ape! It is noon now and you stupid guy are still writing a screenplay for us. Start the play but do shit as you wish."

"Yes sir, but tell me how much money do you want to put for the performance of the screenplay?"

Tony was absorbed in thinking.

The prodigy continued, "Look, there are some points that you must pay attention at. It isn't a one-day film. The film must be played for just a couple of hours. It must seem thoroughly real. It is also a prompt measure and the rest of the story..."

Tony looked at Jones and then at me. While he raised his forefinger directly upward, he said, "One hundred thousand dollars and not more."

I was thinking about the rate, one hundred thousand dollars...one hundred thousand dollars for a one-day film or according to the prodigy, a film for just a couple of hours... one hundred thousand for four of us.

Sometimes a play is performed exactly in front of you but you can't make a head or tail of it, why? Exactly like what a juggler performs in front of you. He stands in front of you and you can see every movement clearly. He even encourages you by the way he acts and talks in order to make you watch his performance with more attention lest you might lose a movement. You struggle so much to find that magic moment, place or movement but you can't. They were also doing magic just like a juggler in front of me.

But the T2 operation was still important. They might intend to avert my thoughts away from the operation by bringing up issues like the money for this mission. But it wasn't possible. The play became more complicated and ridiculous each and every moment. They could easily kill Sara and me and this happening could considerably reduce the rate for at least less two graves. But it seemed they were doing their utmost to rescue four of us with no discrimination among us. I felt like a doll that has no control of it and just waits to be moved by the threads which have been tied to its arms and legs. And in this way, it can feel it is alive.

I hated that situation. I felt so depressed and all in that I was ready to kill myself. But Sara... Sara... Sara...I looked at the building. They were inside and I didn't know what was happening in there.

"Look, so we start the play", the prodigy said it and then got up and continued, "Please get ready for the departure."

Jones asked, "Don't you think Liza makes trouble by her physical condition?"

The prodigy said, "I found a way for it before. Don't worry. We can't omit Liza. If we do it, it takes more time. You four must be killed together. Liza must be transferred by trunk."

Jones said: "Trunk?"

Tony was laughing loudly and Jones was looking at both of them with astonishment.

Jones continued, "You are surely making a joke."

"No, look Jones, it isn't a joke at all. I have nothing to do with joke when I am at work.

But buddy, how can we move Liza with a trunk? Don't laugh Tony Bear. Last night, you were witness that how she was angry about being within the car trunk."

Tony said, "Don't worry. It is on me. I make her accept."

Tony went towards the building and said, "Beautiful Liza, where are you? I have a word with you. Beautiful Liza..."

******

The operation started as we four were chased by two agents appointed by Tony. The operation or as they said, the play was schemed in six stages:

At the first stage, we were observed on one of the highways of the city. Then two agents who identified us started to chase us.

At the second stage, they were trying to find the fourth person who was Liza and it was announced to Tony's commanding center.

At the third stage, the two agents used specific cameras in order to watch inside the car as well as the trunk. Then they found Liza in the trunk.

At the fourth stage, we found that we were chased so we entered the city in order to lose them. Then we got into the traffic, got out of the car and entered the metro station. The metro cameras also filmed us at that time.

At the fifth stage, we got out of the train in another metro station. Then we pulled out a driver out of his Toyota Van, got into the Van and moved towards the beach.

At the sixth stage, we were traced by satellite until we reached the beach. Then we went towards a speedboat that we had hired it before.

When we got into the speedboat, Tony's agents found us. Then there would be conflicts and shooting. Then the chasing would be continued on the ocean to prevent anybody to be injured. Then we went to the bottom of the speedboat and we entered a small submarine by passing through an opening. And then boom...

The boat was exploded by Tony's forces and we escaped by the submarine. It was supposed strong explosive to be installed within the speedboat that vanished the speedboat thoroughly after the explosion. But the important point was how could the play be performed in action?

All four got into the car. Liza was in a trunk within the car trunk. Tony's agents were in another car. I drove towards the city. I had to shop from a supermarket and gas up before reaching the city in order to be identified. Jones and I became aware of all events by the hands free devices that were in our ears through which we could either hear all conversations or talk so we could be aware of any problem or discuss any matter via it.

All those events had to be performed in order to be posed as a document for Tony by which he could claim his wage from the organization. I thought of myself that how much he was going to claim from the organization for killing us? It was an issue that I didn't think about it before. I just thought that our lives were so important for him that he was ready to pay one hundred thousand dollars for a four-hour or five-hour mission. And now I was thinking that how much this bastard was going to take from the organization that he was ready to pay one hundred thousand dollars for this play.

I got out of the car. I heard a tough voice in the hands free, "From agent one to the commanding center. We are chasing a car with three people in it. The driver got out of the car. He must be David Darabont as he has the same feature within the picture."

Tony asked, "Three? No idiots. They must be four. It might be a mistake."

"I don't think so. Can we start?"

Tony said, "No, no. They must be four. Don't take any measure until we get sure about the presence of the fourth individual. No measure, just keep on chasing until we get sure about the fourth one."

I shopped from a supermarket and got back into the car. The next move was that we stopped at a petrol station near the city to take Liza to a toilet. I stopped there and Jones took out Liza from the car trunk. He put the trunk on the ground with caution. Sara took Liza to the toilet.

I heard another voice. He said, "The agent number two is speaking. They stopped at a petrol station. As we are comparing them with the pictures, they are David Darabont, Jones Janatan, Sara Costner but no forth individual...besides there is a suspicious issue."

Tony asked, "What is suspicious, bastards?"

I was filling the tank with petrol.

The first agent said, "The suspicious case is the transferring of a trunk which is moved with caution and Sara took it to the toilet."

Tony said, "Well idiots. She took the trunk with herself because she might need some personal effects."

The first agent said, "The weight of the trunk isn't normal because Jones took it out of the car with difficulty. Even he helped Sara for moving it."

Tony asked, "Well pieces of nothing, what can be inside the trunk?"

After a short silence a voice said, "The agent number two is speaking. It might be ridiculous but the fourth individual might be within the trunk. According to the report, the fourth individual is paralyzed so it doesn't defy common sense if she is put within the trunk to be transferred easier during the escaping operation. It justifies the moving of trunk into the toilet. We just have a professional camera for seeing inside the trunk."

Tony said, "Shit on you. Take it from the car trunk; within the blue box with the code 112001."

When I was filling the petrol tank, I saw one of the agents who got out of the car, opened the car trunk and then returned into the care. Sara came out of the toilet with the trunk. She was stretching the trunk with difficulty. Jones went to help her and put the trunk again into the car trunk.

"Agent number one is speaking. The trunk ingredients have been observed. Someone is within the trunk. The image was sent."

Tony said, "Shit, so the forth one is in there."

The agent number one asked, "Do we have the permission for the car explosion?"

Tony said, "Not yet idiots. I don't want a car explosion to be reflected in news and people to be injured. They are definitely going to escape by the ocean. There is a better opportunity to fix them up there."

Jones was listening the whole conversation on the hands free. He looked at me and said, "Everything is going on well. Now we must go through the bypath for performing the next plan."

I found the bypath on the map. I took more speed and turned into the bypath.

The agent number one said, "They turned into a bypath with high speed. They might be aware of our chasing."

Tony said, "Be careful clumsy guys. Go after them with a close distance from them because we are near the city. It isn't possible to chase them by helicopter."

I turned into the highway again and increased my speed. Now it became more like a real escaping.

The agent number one said, "They surely noticed us."

Tony said, "Dump guy, not important; just keep on going. As I said they would probably go through the bypath towards the ocean."

I turned on the right indicator to enter the highway which was led to the beach.

The agent number two said, "I think your guess is right. The target is the ocean."

All of a sudden I turned my direction towards the town.

The agent number one said, "But it seems we made a mistake. They changed their way towards the city again."

Tony said, "Idiot! They turned their way to lose you within the hustle and bustle of the city. Be all eyes and ears."

I speeded up more and more but I had to keep on at a speed that not to attract the police. I looked at Sara in the front mirror. She was hugging her knees and chewing her nails. Jones permanently looked back and ahead. We entered the city. I kept on driving at high speed. We went towards the metro station. The car which was chasing us got stock within the traffic and took distance from us. We got out of the car within the traffic of the street close to the metro station and escaped through the metro station.

The agent number one said, "They got into the metro station. We got out of the car and are chasing them."

Tony said, "Be careful not to grapple with them. Just chase them. Be also careful about passing people not to be injured. If someone dies, we must pay a dear price for it."

We all three ran and Jones was carrying the trunk with difficulty on his shoulders. The sweat was running off his head and face. As soon as we reached the platform, the train came. We got onto the train. The doors had been closed before the two agents reached the doors and the train moved.

The agent number two said, "We didn't reach on time. The train left."

Tony said, "Shit on you. I chase them by the metro cameras. Come back to your car and wait for my next order."

I looked at Sara. She was still chewing her nails. She was tired. Her eyes grasped my look. She shook her head out of feeling sorrow and stared at a point.

The metro was busy and we stood up. I looked at Jones. He looked agitated. His look conveyed the warning of danger. I traced her look and turned back rapidly. Two people seemed suspicious to me. Jones looked at me again and I got his look's code.

"Tony, I think something is wrong", Jones said as he was looking at me.

Tony asked, "What does it mean?"

Jones said, "I think we have guests."

Tony asked, "Don't you make a mistake?"

I said, "No. I confirmed it too. Anyway we will get off the train at next station. It is better."

The train stopped. We got off the train and went towards the exit door. Jones was watching them stealthy to check if they were still after us.

He looked at me and said, "I don't make a mistake Tony. What must we do now?"

Tony said, "It is ridiculous. They are definitely from another team but how could they find you?"

After a short silence, Tony said, "Nothing. We must continue. It has been like a play so far but it will be real from now on later."

When we got out of the metro station, we moved fast towards the red Toyota Van. I got out my Colt and threatened the driver to get out. People were frightened and they escaped or hid somewhere. We all got into the car and escaped as fast as was possible.

I asked Jones, "Do you think we must keep on with the previous plan?"

Tony said, "Yeah, we have no change in our plan. Just follow the schemed plan. Don't worry about them. I order my forces to fix them up."

We got out of the city. We went towards the beach and four cars were after us but as far as we knew, just one of them was Tony's force.

I said, "I think four cars are after us but just one of them is Tony's force."

Tony was listening to what I was saying to Jones.

He shouted, "No problem. Keep on with your work, ape. You just do as we planned. I know what to do with the other guys."

I looked back. The cars were racing and trying to divert each other from the main path. Then I heard a huge sound from behind. My eyes were on the road. Jones looked back and said, "One went to hell!"

I looked at the back seat in the front mirror. Sara bent over out of fear with the trunk in front of her legs. Now there were three cars behind us, one blue, one red and one black. The black car which was driven by Tony's forces was in conflict with the red one. The blue car which diverted the other car moments ago, speeded up, outpaced from the right shoulder of the road and came in front of the red car. Someone came out of the ceiling of the blue car and aimed the red car with Bazooka. By hearing the explosion, I pressed the accelerator. Now it was just the blue car and the black car that were in no conflict anymore and it indicated that they were both Tony's forces.

Jones turned back and asked loudly," Are you fine my dear?"

Liza said from inside, "I know what to do when I go out."

Jones smiled. Then he looked at Sara and asked, "How are you Sara?"

Sara didn't say anything. Both cars speeded down to give us more time to escape. We reached the beach. We got out of the car. We ran towards the speedboat. A man was waiting there. He helped us to get into the boat. Then he stood behind the steering wheel and pulled down the lever completely. When the boat speeded up, Jones went towards the man and threw him into the water. They shot us from the beach. The other forces also reached the beach but they couldn't do anything. We were riding for about five minutes. It was the last stage but it seemed it took a long time.

Jones asked, "What about the next stage Tony? We are waiting for it."

Tony was silent. Then I noticed that a helicopter was coming towards us from the beach.

Jones yelled, "Hide somewhere, hide somewhere; it isn't our helicopter."

The helicopter barraged us before we could have the smallest move. Jones who was riding the speedboat lost his control and gave a sharp movement to the speedboat. Helicopter passed over our heads and Sara fell down on the deck. First I thought the shaking of the boat caused it but then I noticed her waist was bleeding. I was petrified. Sara was shivering and looked at me with thorough astonishment. She was shocked.

Jones shouted," Damn on you Tony! Sara has been shot. Sara has been shot."

The helicopter which had passed over our heads, turned back towards us. I heard the sound of a helicopter from the beach again.

Tony said, "I think you saw our forces now."

Jones said, "Yeah damn bear! I am seeing but it is late. It is late damn."

I pulled Sara into the cabin. I was crying and Sara was staring at me. I felt dizzy and absent-minded. I found a piece of cloth and put it on the right side of her waist which was shot. I pressed the cloth to impede the bleeding. I was ashamed of myself. I pulled the machine gun out of the sack and got out of the cabin. Farther away, the helicopters were in conflict. One of them exploded.

I looked at Jones. His face was happy and it meant that our helicopter won the battle. Jones adjusted the lever on the automatic mode and we went together inside the boat. Sara was on the ground with open eyes. Jones and I were petrified. Sara was dead. She died for me, for my folly. My feet became listless. I fell down on my knees. I put her head on my chest. I was screaming and crying. Everything was finished for me. Jones was also screaming and uttered words that weren't clear to me in that situation. I didn't hear and understand anything. He opened a valve and pointed to it. He yelled that we had to get down. He threw down Liza's trunk. I didn't want to leave Sara. Everything was finished for me. What did life mean without Sara? Nothing. I was keeping tight to Sara and screaming.

Something like needle pierced my arm and I passed out.

In the state of unconsciousness, all moments of making love with Sara passed through my mind. It was mountain,

Sara and I. Whenever I took part in difficult operations and was witness of unpleasant scenes which put my mind under pressure, I went to the mountains. Mountain was the only place could relax me. While I was climbing, I used to both sing and listen to songs. I thought about what happened and cried loudly.

I got to know Sara when once I came back from the Afghanistan operation and went to the mountains. The Afghanistan operation was like a nightmare. We entered Afghanistan territories to rescue some English commandoes. Everything was schemed and programed. We got off a helicopter to go on foot about a couple of kilometers in a desert to reach the operation region. We reached there but we didn't see anything there. There was neither a military basement nor a house to attack it. Jones was the commander in chief in that operation. He explained to us that the hide-out was under the ground and there was just one way to reach it. He explained that we had to build another path to enter the hide-out. Jones described the situation precisely and we turned on the Giant Excavator Cockroach. It was a device with one meter diagonal which dug the ground and moved forward. It could be adjusted to work slowly or fast. As we didn't know what was going on in there inside the hide-out, we decided to move with the lowest speed to be cautious because the noise might betray our operation. It took two hours to dig the ground with the possible lowest noise. Jones and I checked the movement of the device by radar. When the sensor of the device informed us of being close to the hide-out, Jones stopped the device. Then he turned on the return button. The device pushed out the excavating dust and moved ahead. Finally the device came out and made a tunnel for us. I was appointed to enter the tunnel. I compared what I saw in radar with the map of the hide-out. We were going to enter the hide-out from the end part of that place. I entered the tunnel. It was a steep slope. When I got to the end of the tunnel, I started to dig slowly, with a knife, the remained distance to reach the place. As I had to be cautious, it took about half an hour for me to extract the remained excavated dust. I knew the ceiling of the hide-out might collapse so I tried my best to prevent it somehow. Then I could easily hear the voice of talking and whining but they weren't clear.

Jones said on the phone, "Report the situation."

I said quietly, "Sir, I am very close to the place. I hear some voices. It is not possible now to go inside. We must wait.

Jones said, "Stay there. I will send you the rod-binocular."

They sent the rod-binocular. Its head was equipped with a binocular through which you could clearly see everywhere. I pierced it slowly through the ground. After moving down for about some centimeters, its way became open and Jones was able to watch there by display. I also watched by my own binocular.

It was a small room. There wasn't enough light so we couldn't recognize if the people in there were the captives or the Afghan rebels. But just through that faint light, I recognized that some people were on the ground and didn't move.

The door of the room was opened and the light lit the room. There were some people in English military uniforms who were injured and were in bad condition. A man in Afghani cloth entered the room with a hatchet in his hand and he could speak English well.

He said, "Well dear friends. I came. I came to do as I promised before. Your forces didn't set free our captives and we must send them a present to make them understand we are not joking."

Two more people entered with guns in their hands. They stood behind the man with the hatchet. The fourth person was a young guy with a camera in his hand and the light of his camera made the room lighter. I kept my breath. I didn't dare to move within that dark, narrow and tight tunnel that was just like a grave because the ceiling might collapse and I might be killed.

The man with the hatchet took one of the English forces, pulled him up and put him on the table in the middle of the room. It was like a corpse that was thoroughly disabled. The other captives were almost listless and just their whining could be heard. The man raised the hatchet and brought it down on his arm. I kept my Colt tightly in my fist and mashed it harshly on the ground. The ceiling collapsed and I intruded the room with my head, neck and arms and killed all of them before they could move.

Jones asked, "What a hell are you doing?"

I didn't say anything. I leaped over the floor with my head. Some people were talking outside and they were approaching the room. I shot the first guy outside the door. He fell down and the others who were behind him escaped. They were shooting and running away.

I said, "Major Jones, I think they are moving towards the exit door."

I didn't hear any answer. I heard the sound of shooting from a far distance. I knew that the rebels were terrified and probably entangled in conflict with our forces. I had to go and clear the place. Someone jumped down from the tunnel. It was Major Jones. His head and face was covered with sweat and dust just like me. I was terrified when he opened his blue eyes after coming down.

He said, "Let's go."

We went out of the room. There were two more rooms. There was also a small corridor with a ladder in the end of it that led to the exit door. I opened the first door with my kick. No one was there. I opened the second door with my kick too and saw a scene that made me petrified. James came forward and looked inside the room. One of the English female forces was lying on the table. They cut off their breasts and pierced barbed wire within her vagina. One of her hands was separated from her body and one of her legs was broken and was hanging from the table.

Jones regarded the operation successful but I didn't have the same idea. He believed we were able at least to rescue some commandoes.

I couldn't forget the image of that English female commando. I permanently thought how could that woman bear so much torcher and persecution? When we returned from the mission, the psychologist of the organization prescribed strong medicine for me.

The medicine made me fall asleep and unconscious. After a while I didn't use them anymore and still remembering that scene made me feel sick. I got leave permission for illness and stayed at home all the time. I was dying and the only way was to go to the mountains.

I was singing songs or listening to music and was laughing or crying aloud like nuts. Once I was sitting on the edge of a rock precipice and beneath my feet was empty. I was thinking what would happen if I fell down? Why was I alive? Why did I have to see such a scene? I was dizzy and confused. Jumping down was salvation and freedom for me. I was ready to jump when I noticed someone was climbing down the rock towards where I was sitting. She had a rope on her shoulder and some hooks on her waist that indicated she was a professional climber.

When she reached me, she said, "Be careful. Someone is sitting here."

She stepped on the rock which I was sitting on. The wind was swaying her hair and her eyes...as if I was seeing the image of sea in her eyes.

She smiled and looked at me with more attention. She asked me, "Are you fine?"

I didn't say anything. She surely felt I was on the verge of crying and noticed the drops of tears in my eyes. I was absorbed with her eyes.

Someone behind us asked, "Do we come down the same way Sara?"

Sara looked up and said loudly, "No, not this direction. This rock is just for two people."

She sat beside me. Then she looked down and said, "I hope you weren't thinking about jumping down."

I looked down and said, "Yes, I was thinking about the same thing."

Sara said, "Well, you surely intended to reach down sooner but it isn't the right way."

I said, "No, I wanted to reach the end sooner by jumping."

She said, "But you have a long way to reach the end. Many people are waiting for you before you reach the end."

I smiled and said, "Nobody is waiting for me."

She said, "Well, find someone to wait for you."

Someone asked loudly, "Sara, where are you? We are worried for you."

Sara said loudly, "Don't worry for me. I am sitting here. Have a rest. I have found a friend in here."

She looked at my muscular body which was showing off under my t-shirt.

Then she smiled at me and said, "If you want, I will wait for you in there. So now you have someone who will be waiting for you down in there. So despite of reaching the end, reach down. Going down doesn't always mean falling down. Do you promise me to come down to see me in there?

I nodded.

She said, "It isn't enough. Promise me."

I said, "I promise."

She asked, "What do you promise?"

I said, "I promise to reach down not to reach the end...for seeing you."

She smiled, got up and said, "I will be waiting for you."

I was going down and down to reach Sara. It was like climbing a rock with difficulty. Her face and smile was in front of my eyes. Her voice was in my ears and I still felt the smell of her body's sweat.

Sometimes when I came back from football and took off my clothes, my mother kept them tight to her face and smelled them before putting them in the washing machine.

I asked, "Why do you do it mum? They have bad odor."

My mother smiled and said, "Whenever you like the smell of someone's body you must know that you love it and I love you. Do you understand?"

I said, "Yes, I understood."

She said, "No, you don't understand until you fall in love."

At that time I found that I fell in love with her and my other experiences in having feelings towards someone before wasn't love. Later I found that Sara had the very specifics which were my favorite ones. Grief and bad events are always in your life but you must have someone in your life whom by seeing them, by talking with them, by kissing them or by touching them, you forget everything.

Sara, being shot, boat...all of them attacked my mind abruptly. I opened my eyes. The first thing I felt was a weird headache and eye ache. My eyesight became dark and blear.

Tony was yelling on the phone, "If I ever lay my hands on your bastard boss, I will pierce a post in his asshole in order to make him understand not to behave us like this next time. He said that he just hired me but there were two more groups for this mission. I was going to lose my forces. Just tell him my message and tell him add ten percent to the payment. I agreed on the rate of payment in case no one else interfered but the presence of the other groups increases the rate. Tell him my message to make him understand how he should behave when he orders a mission. Dirty bastards!"

He cut off the phone. I was gasping. Tony didn't notice that I came round. Jones was sitting a bit far. Liza wasn't there. I was lying on a sofa and there was a Colt on a table close to me. I moved my hand towards the Colt but moving my hand was as difficult as lifting an object of one hundred kilos. First I tried to aim it at Jones and then start talking but my hand was listless. I put it on my chest and put my finger on the trigger but I knew that I wasn't even able to press the trigger. Tony turned back and looked at me.

"Hey buddy! Did you come round?"

"Don't move Jones. Just don't move."

"What are you doing David?"

"Why did you put the Colt on your throat?"

Tony came and stood beside him.

"Where is Sara?"

Tony and Jones looked at each other.

Jones said, "I am sorry David but you know..."

"Yes I know. Where is her corpse?"

"We didn't bring the corpse. It was left in the boat and the helicopter exploded the boat. We are really sorry David."

My head got hot. I felt the blood was boiling in my head. I wanted to yell but I had no voice. My breath was hot and tears were running my eyes. Tony tried to approach.

"Don't move bastard. Don't move."

"Jones said, "What are you doing David? Control yourself."

"Control myself!? Sara died...do you understand?...just for me..." I said while I was sobbing.

I whimpered loudly. I put the muzzle under my throat and pressed the trigger with all my strength. The Colt was empty.

Tony faced Jones and said, "I told you that it takes a long time..."

I passed out again. When I opened my eyes, I was lying on bed. It was like a hospital room rather than a house room. I was dizzy for a while. I didn't know where I was, why I was there and what happened. I tried to lot to move but I couldn't. I was afraid. I could move my head a little but moving the rest of my body was impossible. My eyes were blear and burning a little. I remembered the scene of Sara's death again. I shouted and shouted again and again.

The door was opened and Liza entered the room with wheelchair. She seemed sad. She came beside my bed. I was on the verge of tears. She kept my hand in her both hands but I couldn't even feel her hands.

"What happened to me? Was I shot? Why can't I move? Did I become crippled?"

"Calm down David. Don't worry. Everything will be ok."

I was gasping lest I might get paralyzed.

I said, "Every...everything...everything will be ok? Oh, my God! What do you mean everything will be ok? Sara is dead. Sara left this world. How will everything be ok? Ok, bring her back then everything will be ok."

Tears made Liza's face wet. She was rubbing the back of my hand on her cheek.

"I am really sorry David. I am really sorry."

"Why can't I move? Damn with it. What happened to me?"

Jones and the prodigy entered the room. They stood on both sides of my bed.

Jones said, "How are you David?"

I looked at him and said, "I am good...very good...can't you see? I feel awesome...awesome but I don't know why I can't move. My eyes are blear. I can't breathe well."

The prodigy said, "Don't worry. Nervous attack made you like this. It takes a while until you get normal.

I yelled, "How long?"

The prodigy said, "Look David...don't worry...calm down."

"You dirty bastard guy, don't tell me calm down again and again. Could you be calm if you were in my shoes?"

"Tell me Jones, Could you be calm if Liza died?"

"No."

"So why are you telling me to calm down all of the time?"

Liza said, "We are all really sorry..."

"What is the use of being sorry?"

The prodigy faced Jones and said, "We tried to help them but now this is what we get in return for our help. If we hadn't got involved in this story, they both would have been killed."

I shouted, well, "You had better let us die and the story was over. Why didn't you let? Too many troubles and too much expenditure for us...whyyy?"

Liza said, "Because we have a great target and we needed both of you."

I kept silent and let her continue talking.

"All we have done has been for humanitarianism not just for two people with the names of David and Sara. We wanted you both to be with us and although Sara died but we are happy you are still alive."

I said, "What can I do for you? What is the big target that you put yourselves into so much trouble? What can a target mean to me now that Sara is dead?"

Liza looked at Jones. Jones shrugged and said, "It is better we go. You tell him everything."

They left the room. Liza let go of my hand and pushed her wheelchair towards the window. She opened the curtain and gazed at a point through the window.

"Many years ago, when I was working in the intelligence service, our sense of being nosey sometimes rose and we became naughty. I had a colleague, Kathrin. We were friends and the same age. One of the senior officials of the intelligence service proposed her but their age difference was too much. He was eighteen years older that Kathrin. I tried to advise her that if she wanted to live with him, she had better not care the age difference. Kathrin made excuses in order to think over it. According to George's file at the organization, he didn't get married before. They went out together a couple of times. After a while, Kathrin became suspicious about his calls and absence. Our sense of being nosey rose and we decided to bug out his calls.

He always had short talks regarding the operations and gatherings with the officials of the organization. There was no sign of another woman in his life. We kept on wiretapping until he ordered the prompt performance of an operation in one of his calls. The first suspicious issue was that the order was done on the phone while most operations were usually confirmed during a gathering or at least an online session.

It wasn't still too unusual. Anyway there were too many secret operations that were reported later to the information recording section of the organization in which we worked. But we didn't receive any report regarding the operation which George talked about. This issue made us suspicious. First we thought that the operation was surely a long one and that is why we didn't receive its report. We tried to find which operation took place at that time and where in this world. But the less we found as the more we researched about it and the more curiosity could kill the cat. It has been about two or three years that I lived with Jones and he was the only one I could trust him. So I told him everything."

I said, "So it also happened to you."

"Exactly and I told him everything. As Jones became aware of more suspicious events, he also became curious about this issue. So he asked us to continue our wiretapping and we did as he said. Three operations were announced by him through just one month but none of them were recorded in the organization while I knew the individual who received the orders. He was the United Nation's agent for performing specific operations. Well when both the commander and the performer were the members of the United Nation and no information was recorded within the organization, this issue made us more curious and sensitive. Jones asked us to record all the conversations and provide documents as much as we could. Jones didn't also tell us about important issues that he found. Jones was tracing this issue by Tony secretly. Tony was one of the senior officials of the organization and in spite of this issue that he was aware of all events within the organization but he didn't also have any information about this operation. Nobody could find what the play was. It wasn't also right to enter the play and interpolate them. With no doubt it was an unusual scheme and we might prove nothing by revealing it. It might also put us into trouble that it did."

"Well, how did you get into trouble?"

"All of our researching was betrayed. We all four trusted each other and no one else cooperated with us in this regard. But the issue that who traced our activities was all Greek to me. One night Tony called Jones and said something that made him sick."

I asked, "What happened Jones?"

"He said that Kathrin was kept captive. I asked him Kathrin! Captive! Who? Where? And as Tony said, the astonishing issue was that we had to go there otherwise they would kill her.

You can't imagine how difficult the time was passing by. Tony, Jones and I went to the place where they asked us to go. I was nagging all the time that it was the most foolish act we could do. Why should we give up? But if we hadn't gone there, Katherine would have been killed and if we had gone there, we all would have been killed. So there was no use of going there. But Tony insisted that we had to go and he was right. It needed too courage that wasn't my job. Just Tony and Jones were brave enough to do that. We went to a desolate factory. George was there. Kathrin was also there while sitting on a chair with fastened arms and legs."

Liza was on the verge of crying and her chin was shivering. I couldn't stand anymore. While I was pressed my teeth together, I said, "Please, go on."

Kathrin was beaten savagely. Her jaw was displaced and her eyes were so swollen that couldn't open them.

Jorge said, "Well, give us the all documents...all recorded wiretapping."

Tony laughed and said, "I hand them over with all my pleasure."

George put the muzzle of the Colt on Kathrin's head and shot. Just like that.

Liza burst into crying and breathed with difficulty.

"I...was astonished...I didn't know...the reason of so much atrocity. We all three were frightened. George's forces surrounded us with their guns and we put ourselves into a plight... with no defending equipment. I thought it was the end of our lives. George aimed his gun at me and said, "You the next one if I didn't cooperate." Jones was standing in front of me. Then I hear sounds. Two forces fell on the ground. George was scared. He abruptly ordered for shooting. That place turned into a hell, a real hell. First I thought they were the organization's forces but I made a mistake. Then I found that they were Tony's forces who came there with his coordination."

"You mean the forces that protected you weren't the forces of the organization?"

"No."

"So, where were they from?"

"They were Tony's forces. In those years, he was trying to employ private forces and nobody was aware of that even Jones."

"You mean the same forces who are still working for him now?"

"Yes."

"I still feel dizzy. The more you say about those events, I become dizzier and my head gets hot. My paralyzed body also makes me more agitated and nobody can understand me."

"I understand you David. I have been sitting on a wheelchair the best years of my life. I thoroughly understand what you say. Your condition is temporary but I must be on this wheelchair whole my life."

"Well, tell me the rest of the story. But please, don't make it more complicated."

"In that conflict, a bullet hit my waist and made me like this."

I whimpered and said, "Oh, my God. Why are you evading? George, those events, the unrecorded operation, what about them?"

Liza shouted, "Tony? Hey Tony Bear?"

"Yes, beautiful Liza."

"Come here. You must tell the rest of the story."

"The rest of the story? Which story?"

"I want you to tell David what exactly happened in the organization. Depict exactly everything for him."

"Why should I explain everything for David? Why do you and Jones want David to know everything?"

Liza moved her wheelchair and faced Tony. Then she said aloud and clearly, "Do as I said and don't ask any question. Answer all his questions. That is all."

Tony shrugged and said, "Yes beautiful mam."

Tony came near my bed. He put a chair beside my bed and sat on it. He took a deep breath and said," I am at your service. Ask me?"

"Tony I am at the end of my rope. Please explain everything."

"I don't know what must I explain about?"

"Liza told me about the events during which Kathrin was killed and Liza was shot, but she didn't say what happened to George."

He fisted his hand and hit on his other hand's palm many times. He yawned and asked, "What is the use of it for you? We suppose you know the whole story; what is the use of knowing it? You wanted to kill yourself."

"Tony, I lost my love. You must understand me. But I want to find an excuse for living. I feel that all those events might give me a motivation for taking revenge for Sara."

"If you think so, that is ok; I tell you what happened. But you must know that being aware exactly of what happened embraces two issues – first it might put your life into danger and second it depends on you ape to believe it or not. Bu I tell you everything exactly as it happened. After Liza and Kathrin found what was going on. They told Jones about it and then Jones conveyed it to me. In fact Jones and I had a secret connection. Not every Tom, Dick and Harry knew about the secret connections in the organization. In fact I had to have this secret connection with Jones to gain information from the other commanders for performing the missions which were recommended to us.

After permanent chasing, we found that George was one of the senior officials of the United Nations and some operations had taken place under his direct order while each operation had to be confirmed by at least three officials of the intelligent service as well as the researching center. So some operations took place but there was no report for them. Then we found that those operations didn't take place on the direction of the United Nations' aims."

"What do you mean that those operations didn't take place on the direction of the United Nations' aims?"

"Ok, I explain clearly. Resume that you enjoy a legal full authority. Then you decide to use this authority for your own benefits. It is enough to deal with some guys and then represent justifications. Then everything will be ok."

"Tony we were in the organization too. These shit events which you are talking about cannot take place in the United Nations."

"I told you before that it depend on you if you accepted it or not. But we also took it serious when we found that the United Nations was just a shit place...I mean a public WC."

"How did they benefit from those operations?"

"The operations were performed for different reasons. The soldiers didn't doubt anything. I mean they weren't aware of the organization's aims. For example, why were you dispatched for the T2 operation?"

"We were dispatched to rescue some doctors and nurses who were sent there for help by the organization but they were kept captive."

"Tony guffawed and mashed his palm on his lap. His reaction made me nervous but I preferred to be silent. He stopped laughing."

"Yes, your aim was rescuing the doctors and the nurses. Almost all individuals who work for the organizations are great and self-sacrificed people. But there was no doctor or nurse in there."

"So why did we go there?"

"The truth is that they played with you. You were dispatched as the special forces of the organization to rescue the hostages. But this mission wasn't ordered by the organization. They put a record of leave permission for all of the solders of your team but you weren't aware of that. On the other hand you had to do your mission...secretly...so you were sent there by the organization but without their knowledge."

"So what was the operation for if it wasn't for rescuing?"

"Just one word has always had a key role for Africa. This country has always been in poverty and its people have taken for slavery for just one thing – diamond, diamond and again diamond and besides the rich resources which exist in this continent has been the other reason. But this continent must be kept as a hungry continent so as that the capitalists profit more and more. You were being played by them. You went there under the command of the bastard Daggles Cliff to deal diamond and come back. And the significant point was that you were supposed to receive diamond in return for giving drugs. It was a profitable deal and also suggestive. You went there but the plan changed in the middle of your mission. Many groups were after that diamonds which were supposed to be sold. One of them was Dancy, the very White whom you saw in there, a real bastard. They came there for the diamonds and the head of the tribe got away from the village. So no deal could be performed and that was why your mission was canceled."

"I ask a question and I want an answer."

"Ask."

"Do you know who was leading T2?"

"I know him well."

"Well, why don't you take a measure? Why are you silent?"

"Well, listen ape. The story that I told you was one of the easiest play they schemed. There are more complicated plays that we must find their secrets so we must be silent presently otherwise all our efforts will go to nowhere. If we cut their roots at this stage, no more we can learn about the more hidden ones. We must wait and see how deep those roots are penetrating and when we reach the bottom of the root, then boooommmm. We fix up them all. I told you everything which was necessary and that's over."

"He got up and went towards the door of the room while he was limping. But before leaving the room he turned back and said, "You were never able to find the secret information of the organization if it wasn't our help. If you found that no operation was recorded at the organization's system, it was our job. Someone from the organization told me that you were asking suspicious questions and we tried to make you close to the truth even before you went to see Jones."

Liza looked at me but I didn't like to talk to anyone. Sometimes you have a weird feeling. While you are suffering from the biggest grief of the world, you want to laugh from the bottom of your heart. But you don't do it because you might be shy of the grief you have in your heart. Sometimes just like when you eat something heavy and it can't be digested, you have something in your mind and it is rasping on your nerves. The problem is that to resolve your digestion problem, you can put your finger into your throat and vomit whatsoever you ate, but what can you do for what can't leave your mind.

Episode Three

Jones and Tony were torturing the prodigy about six hours from and ten past eleven at night to ten past five in the morning. It was a full-scale torturing; a real barbarian atrocity. Nobody told me what happened. But as I knew Jones and Tony well, I knew that there was a reason for that. The prodigy didn't defend himself and it proved that they were right. But as I knew the prodigy, he couldn't do something wrong that made them behave him like that.

They used electricity, iron, injection, and needle. They even pressed his eggs but none of them made him talk. Although he was named "the prodigy" for his unique program planning and performance as well as network influencing technics but he was also peerless in not giving information.

I couldn't do anything. They didn't tell me what happened. I reviewed all recent events in my mind unit I might find the answer for it. The prodigy and I came to Iran after the New York events; the country which I didn't know anything about. Just I heard that they butchered any foreigner came to that country. I heard that if a woman didn't wear scarf, the government would cut off her head. I also heard that in Iran's prisons, hooligans carried gun which seemed to be ridiculous.

When I told the prodigy about what I heard about Iran, he laughed and said, "I am also Iranian. There are also hooligans, thieves, drug traffickers and bastards in Iran like the other countries. But using gun in Iran is something different and hanging you from your eggs is the least they do if you use gun. So forget about gun because for using things like this, the hanging rope is always ready."

Later I found that whatsoever I heard was wrong and Tehran seemed so calm and peaceful.

When we were in the airplane, I asked him softly, "Finding Bin Laden must not be a difficult job for the Iranian security forces with regard to what you are saying about them if he is in Iran as you say. So isn't it ridiculous that you and I are after the biggest fugitive of the world?"

He looked at me and said, "Look buddy. You must shut up from now on later. I am serious. Deadly shut up. Be quiet. Believe me I don't want to pull your leg. But please write on a piece of paper what you want to say in front of others and sometimes you must do the same thing even we are both alone. Did you get?"

I said, "Ok."

He said, "No, you didn't notice. If you had got what I told you, you would just have nodded."

I closed my mouth and nodded. After Sara's death and the way I felt, now big motivations could push me forward.

Now the issue was killing Bin Laden. The mission was to find Bin Laden. Our aim was interesting but it was just Tony Bear, Jones, Liza, the prodigy and I; how could we push the procedure ahead?

We were in a safe house in Iran for some days and I didn't go out at all. Once the prodigy came home and asked me to help him.

I asked, "What kind of help? Did you find something?"

He said, "No, look, I want you to go somewhere to get even with some guys."

I asked, "To get even for what?"

He put a Colt on the table.

I looked at the Colt and said, "But what you said about the security forces in Iran..."

He said, "Don't worry."

And why shouldn't I be worried with regard to what he said about the Iranian security forces; the forces who were like a nightmare for the CIA agents lest they might encounter them or might be taken captive by them. I came to Iran for finding Bin Laden. The mission was like using hallucinogenic drugs for forgetting the absence of Sara. It was difficult but I had to live. I had to take revenge for Sara. After killing Bin Laden I was going to kill the guy who was responsible for T2 operation as well as the death of Sara. So

I wanted to keep on the way that I had chosen and I had to look ahead and use my capabilities to help people. It was a big job and I decided to do it.

By the way how are you? I am talking with you who are reading this text and laugh. Are you surprised? Now what do you think about me? I am the very guy who butchered Daggles Cliff. I hope you didn't forget. As it was difficult for you to clear up the dirty image that you made out of me, it is now difficult for me to explain why I wanted to find Bin Laden in Iran. It was difficult and unbelievable for me to do it but I decided to do it and it was worth doing it.

The prodigy asked me to help him for doing something that had no relevance with killing Bin Laden. It was two and thirty AM. He gave me some explanations about the place that we were supposed to go in order to make me aware of what we were going to do before going there. I thought it was a foolish act. We were after a big aim and he was after something that could keep us aloof from our main goal. We might have been killed but something inside me told that I had better trust him.

We moved from north of Tehran and reached the south border of the city. As we moved further down the city, the number of modern houses and cars was decreasing and we reached more and more the poorer sections of the city.

Watching Tehran at that time of the night made me exited. I watched the villages and deserts of Iran at just some TV reports and films before. It wasn't busy contrary to what it was during the day when we went from the airport to our house and we got stock in the traffic jam.

The prodigy drove into the bank of the road. He turned off the lights and stopped the car about one hundred meters farther ahead. He asked me to get out of the car. I had a Colt and he had a small Beretta. We walked about one hundred meters farther ahead again. I felt danger. I perceived someone's odor easily. Someone was walking along with us on the right direction behind the small heaps of dust. I breathed deeply a couple of times to make Tony aware of the situation. He nodded and kept on going.

Some white conexes could be seen farther ahead. Tony stood where he was facing me and in front of the guy who was chasing us. He said, "shoot him."

Tony dodged and I shot him abruptly. He bit the dust before he could have a smallest reaction.

Why did I shoot him? Why did I do as the prodigy said? What was his crime? What could justify my action? Nobody was chasing us anymore. I was sure. My smelling ability works well in such situations. We were approaching the conexes. There were four. I could smell blood, wine and drug. Three of them had no light and just one was lit along. The sounds of yelling and laughing also could be heard.

I looked through the conex's window. He signed for intruding into the conex. I had to kick the door and then he would enter. I kicked the door so fiercely that the door got out of its frame. He entered and barraged. I heard the voice of a girl who was yelling. I didn't enter. I knew that there was no need of me inside and I had to be cautious. The sound of barrage was stopped but the girl's yelling was still kept on. I entered the conex. Some big bloody lacerated men were on the ground. A girl about twelve was in there too. She had wrapped a piece of cloth around her naked body. She was out of breath by being frightened. She was breathing with so difficulty that she might strike by heart attack. The prodigy said something in Persian. Her breathing ameliorated and then she pointed outside. I broke the lock of one of the conexes and lit it by my porch. Some dirty, weak and listless boys and girls about ten to fifty were sitting on the ground. Their skin was dark but they weren't like the local Tehrani people.

The prodigy talked to them but the only word that I got was, "police". I didn't get why he said it. We went towards the third conex. There wasn't something important in there. It was just a storage. We opened the door of the fourth conex. As soon as we opened it, the flow of chilly weather irritated my face. I felt the smell of more blood. It was like a fridge. It was full of small metal boxes. The prodigy opened one of them. It was kidney. The next box contained heart and...

Why wasn't it right to shoot him? Why wasn't it right to kill that guy? Oh, I wish I would have known him before I had killed him. If I knew whom I was going to kill then I got more pleasure of killing him. Killing dirty men is pleasurable. Oh, damn on me that I say dirty men. Man...what a simple and complicated word!

If we have a deeper look at the issue, why should we consider the dirty creatures that are apparently similar to human being as men? This question has always been in my mind. Was the head of those rebels inT2 a man?

The prodigy sat and cried with loud voice. Seeing the prodigy in that position was too weird for me. I remembered the Black who butchered the children with hatchet at the T2 operation. He cut off the newly borne baby's hands and feet and the baby's father was watching and yelling. He picked up the feet of the baby and kissed their soles. He picked up the hands of the baby and kissed their palms. He was out of breath by sobbing. He picked up the body and kissed the baby's lips.

We all commandoes who were present in there were crying. He put the butchered body of his baby in piece of cloth and yelled while saying some things. We didn't understand what he was saying.

I asked one of the commandoes who was originally African, "What does he say?"

He answered while he was yelling out of sorrow," Why did you come late? What is the use of your coming so late? If you are supposed to come after we are slaughtered, you had better go to hell."

He put the baby in a piece of cloth to dig it beside a tree. He hugged the baby and sat beside the tree. He sang the cradlesong in his own language for the baby and then put it in the hole and covered it with soil. He shouted loudly many times. He got up. He pulled out the knife that he had in his pants stock. First we thought he wanted to attack us. We went backwards some steps. He said something and then he cut his neck with the tip of his knife. The blood splashed out. He did it so fast and sharply that we couldn't stop him. He fell down and died.

The commando who knew his language asked, "Do you know what he said?"

I said, "No."

He said, "You are too late timid chickens. Don't act like heroes. It isn't worth being with you in this world."

And now the prodigy was crying as severely as that black man. I was shivering. I was afraid that lest he might do something foolish just like that black man and kill himself. I kept close to him in order to stop him if he wanted to do something folly. When he kept a little bit calmer, we got up. He took out a gallon out of the storage. He entered the first conex and poured the petrol on the copses.

I asked, "Isn't it better to let them be identified?"

He was looking at the lighter which he was holding in his hand and then put it off. He seemed to have lost all his energy and stamina. He was doddering while walking. He told something to the girl wrapped in a piece of cloth by moving his hands and legs. She nodded but didn't say anything. She was still frightened and shivering. The girl went into the children conex and the prodigy locked it.

He called someone when we were going towards the car. I was angry with him because I didn't understand even a word of his talks. We got into the car and returned the main road. He pulled away the car. Further ahead at far distance, I saw some police cars turn into the bypath. The prodigy closed his eyes and sobbed again. Some minutes later, he started the car and we set off. The sun rose in the sky and its warmth stroked my face. There was no need of his explanation. Everything was clear and I was happy but the issue that why he chose us for doing the job and why he didn't give the mission to the other guys was weird to me. Anyway I didn't like to ask any question.

But after that mission, I believed in the prodigy. He knew the meaning of humanitarianism and was ready to fight for it. That was enough for me to continue with him. Is there something more important than humanitarianism in this world?

It was the only job we did and we didn't do anything else. But even that job couldn't justify Tony and Jones's barbaric behavior.

Tony and Jones came out of the room. Their clothes were wet with sweat. Tony lit a cigar. Jones was gasping. They didn't say anything.

I asked, "Don't you want to talk about your barbaric behavior?"

nobody answered.

I continued, "Jones, do you think is it right to behave like this with someone who saved our lives?"

He finally talked and asked, "Hey buddy, haven't you still learned that doing a job is something different from personal issues?"

Moments later, the prodigy came out of the room while doddering. He was just wearing shorts. All her body and face was bloody and swollen. There was the stain of hot iron on his left chest and his right lap. His fingers were bleeding. One of his eyes was swollen as big as a peach and the other one became squint. He looked at us one by one. Then he opened his arms and guffawed. His mouth was full of blood. He guffawed for some seconds. He went towards Tony, grabbed his cigar from his lips and put it in the corner of his mouth. Now he wasn't shivering; he was trembling. He lay on the sofa and fainted out of pain and listlessness. The cigar remained in the corner of his lips.

Tony asked, "Hey ape, do you know what we are really doing? Do you know what our aim is?"

I said, "As far as I know you were supposed to find Bin Laden. Of course doing such a mission wasn't acceptable for me from the very beginning. Ok, we know that there is someone who is named, Tony and he has a private professional team but what kind of information do you have in comparison with the information of the other countries' intelligence services that can enable you to find Bin Laden? I feel what we are doing is ridiculous somehow."

Tony who seemed furious and blew a fuse said, "And to you it is definitely ridiculous too if I tell you that it has been many years that this damn prodigy knows where he is."

Jones said," And to you it is definitely ridiculous too if I tell you that I sent Saddam into hell before the American forces could find him."

I smirked and said, "So finding Saddam and hanging him..."

Tony said, Saddam? Which Saddam? You mean the old man who was taken out from the bottom of a well? Then there was a TV report in which some people were checking his hair, skin and mouth. Then they apparently brought him into trial and hanged him. Hurrah USA! Hurrah USA, the hero! Hurrah USA, the antiterrorism. Saddam was an American burnt piece that didn't succeed to annihilate Iran so the order of his assassination was issued. It was an

American-English scenario that we shit on it. So they put on show a hanging performance to say that the play was over.

I liked to bring out my Colt and shit their heads. I felt they were making fun of me. Can we ignore all those events and take them just as a play? Do you believe it? Yes, you? How do you feel if someone comes and tell you that you are wrong about something that you are definitely sure about it?

But no, wait a moment. Let's be suspicious. Whatsoever we know about an event is through news. There were some fake people who were Saddam's doubles. How do we know that the person whom they showed us was Saddam? Was he Saddam because the media was telling that? Was it enough?

All their talks at least led me to become suspicious about those events; the events which I believed before and I was sure about them. I sometimes thought Tony and Jones were right and I sometimes thought why should I believe them? Aren't you suspicious about something? If I tell you that Gathafi was killed because he threw away UN human rights book, would it make you laugh? Would it make you laugh again if I tell you that there was no need of those bloody events for arresting Saddam, Gathafi and Bin Laden? Yes, all those issues make us laugh as long as our mind is in the hands of the media and we believe whatsoever they release.

Now it was the shit prodigy, Tony, Jones and I. And the prodigy knew where Bin Laden was.

I asked Tony and Jones, well, "What did you find by so much torturing? Did you succeed to prize something out of him?"

None of them answered. I continued, "How is it possible that someone like the prodigy knows about Bin Laden's place but an organization like the USA Intelligence Service is ignorant about his place?"

Jones answered, "Why do you think they don't know?"

I thought of myself, what did it mean, "Why do you think they don't know?" If they knew it so what were so many plays for? Why was so much bloodshed for finding Bin laden? So many plays...and I was thinking about those words, "so many plays."

Tony said, "He played with us badly. We trusted this bastard for ruining the Americans' play neglecting of the issue that he was also playing with us."

The prodigy was breathing loudly and harsh sounds were heard from his throat. He coughed up blood. He came around. He was looking around while he was dizzy and groggy.

He said, "From now on later...I am the boss. Do you understand? I am the boss...I order everybody what to do."

And he passed out again.

I said," I hope you answer my question this time. If they know where he is so why don't they go and arrest him? And why has the prodigy been silent about his place so far?"

Tony Bear said, "We tortured him to find this but he didn't open his mouth."

****

After some days, the prodigy got all right. We were safe in a house for one week. We were watching TV. The programs weren't good and even if it was good, I didn't understand a word. Going outside was forbidden and we were waiting for an order by the prodigy or the so-called new boss.

After one week, he said, "We all four must come back."

Tony said, "Where the bastard?"

The prodigy said, "New York. We must prepare for the public assembly of UN in 2010. We have got a lot to do there."

Tony puffed his cheeks and said, "Damn with you! Damn with you! We must come back again into that mouse hole. Of course you and me have no problem but what about Jones and David? Isn't it better they stay in Iran? If we want to do something in there concerning the public assembly, we can't use them."

The prodigy said with confirmation, "We must use them. We must."

Tony yelled, "Why don't you understand? I have issued the document of their death and if this secret issue is revealed, no one will trust my private team anymore. Not only I would have no order from anyone but also the other groups take the order of killing me. Do you understand or not?"

Without paying any attention to Tony's furious face as well as his protruded neck's vessels he said, "I understand but both Jones and David must be with us."

Tony didn't say anything anymore. Jones sat beside Tony to calm him and then he said, "I trust him buddy. He surely has a right plan when he insists us to return to New York."

The prodigy said, "Did you see what he said? Jones trusts me. That was why he tortured me so much. Hahaha..."

Tony and Jones didn't say anything anymore. The prodigy went out and came back after a couple of hours. He came back with a bag along with Iranian original passports for Jones and me but with another name and identifications.

I was analyzing the issues. There were many things that were still unclear. There was still another question that how were Jones and Tony still alive after killing that senior official of the UN? Why should Jones and Tony abruptly come to Iran from New York and put their lives into danger just to get information about Bin Laden from the prodigy? Why didn't they wait to see him later?

Tony asked the prodigy, "You knew that Bin Laden wasn't in Iran so why did you come here?"

The prodigy got up and looked out of the window from which Tehran's high-rises could be seen. He kept silent for some moments and without averting his eyes from the window he said, "Well, I missed my homeland. Besides first I had to get even with someone that was a personal retaliation and second I had another mission which was sending Bin Laden's wife and children out of Iran that I did it."

How many times have you been in a situation in which you cannot laugh or cry, you cannot talk to someone or listen to someone, you cannot even get up and walk? When he talked about the exiting of Bin Laden's family, we had such a feeling. Little by little I found that I wasn't the only guy who was astonished by those events and Tony and Jones were like me too. They couldn't make a head or tail of what the prodigy was doing and their silence was indicative of this issue. The prodigy took his laptop and went to the other room. We were just sitting on a sofa and looked at each other for about two hours. We were thinking. We couldn't do anything else in that situation. When I saw Jones and Tony's state of wondering, I couldn't let myself ask even the smallest question. It was just silence, silence and silence. It seemed that the prodigy to become the main boss and even Tony had to obey him.

****

We all four came back to New York; Jones and I with bald heads and fake identifications. My name was Ali and his name was Arash. We were also provided with identification cards introduced us as specific reporters for the 2010 UN General Assembly. We didn't pass through the passport and visa checking gate. Two people in usual cloths took us out of the airport from the other direction. We went to a hotel. We had to wait there for the start of the play of the General Assembly; the play which they arrange every year. "The play of the General Assembly", it was the phrase that I heard from Aboutaleb for the first time. I went again to Aboutaleb's shop next day after I had gone there with my mother for apologizing. His staff wasn't there and he was gazing at the TV. He didn't notice that I came and was listening to a speech which was directly being broadcasted from the TV. He was so absorbed by the speech that he couldn't hear me call him. I waited while I was looking at him. His absorption to the speech was interesting to me. When the speech finished and the audience clapped, he fisted on the table and said, "Damn with all of you. Damn with all of you! This is just a play, a play by the United Nations."

Then he noticed my presence. "He asked, do you need anything?"

I said, "Yes, my mother gave me a list of goods to buy them."

He looked at the list and said, "You can take them from the end of the shop."

I took a step forward, faced Anoutaleb and asked, Aboutaleb! Can I ask a question?

He looked at me and said, "Ask."

I asked, "Why did you curse them?"

He nodded and asked, "How old are you?"

I said, "Twelve."

He said, I am seventy two; It means I live sixty years more than you. Once I lived in my own country. I had a family. I had many relatives. I had a good life. I am older than the United Nations. This organization has been launched for protecting all people around the world. But...but since it started to work, there has been more war and bloodshed in the world. Each year, they come and deliver speeches in the organization. Each country talks about its own problems and complains about the interference of other countries into their own country's affairs but nobody talks about humanity as well as humanitarianism. الله اكبر.

I asked, "What does humanity mean?"

He took a deep breath. Then he thought and said, "David,

humanity can be defined in just one word. If you understand it and believe it, you will be a human being."

I asked, "Just one word?"

He said, "Just one word. Do you know what it is?"

I said, "No."

He said, "Harmlessness. Humanity means harmlessness. If you want to be loved by God, you must be harmless. Even if you don't believe in any religion and even you don't praise God, you are loved by God by being harmless."

I asked, "You mean lying isn't bad? Stealing isn't bad? What about laziness?"

He said, "When you lie, you irritate someone by not telling the truth. When you steal something, you irritate someone. When you do anything bad, you irritate someone. When you are lazy, you put others into trouble and they will be irritated. So humanity is just in one word, harmlessness. Whenever you want to do something first regard if it irritates someone or not. If it doesn't, do it and if it irritates someone, don't do it even if it concerns your own affairs."

I asked, "What does it mean, even if it concerns your own affairs?"

He said, "For example, some people drink alcohol or some others are addicted. When they are advised that what they do isn't right, they say that they don't hurt anyone but they don't know that they are hurting themselves. When they hurt themselves, they lose their humanity. It isn't important if you are Muslim, Christian or laic; what is important is that you must be a good human being. All religions have a common word and it is the matter of being good. Whenever you see a religion whose beliefs and rituals hurt others, it isn't a real religion; it is a fabricated one."

After many years, that dialogue between Aboutaleb and I was just like a recorded tape which was being played in my mind again. "Human, humanity, harmlessness" and I was after them all those years. How easy and what an honorable individual taught me that word and I didn't save it in my mind. Human, humanity, harmlessness. I believe that the biggest secrets of the world are in front of our eyes but they are so close to us that we easily skip them and don't care them. And the secret of humanity was what Aboutaleb said. But really, which word can define humanity better than harmlessness? If you harm others, you aren't a human.

Jones's voice pulled me out of my remembrances.

"What are you thinking about Ali?"

I didn't answer his question and said, "Well, what is our plan now Arash?"

He said, "I don't know exactly but what I know is that it is a job as significant as serving humanity as the prodigy said."

Someone knocked our door. We abruptly took our Colts.

Jones went towards the door and asked, "Who is that?"

"I am a cowboy."

It was Tony's voice. He opened the door. Tony and the prodigy came in. By seeing Jones's bald head, Tony slapped him on the head and said, "You became so handsome bald guy."

The prodigy didn't say anything. He closed the curtains. Cut the phone. Turned off the cell phones and even took out its battery. He stuck a piece of big paper on the wall. He took a marker and wrote, just shut up. Stop blasphemy. Then he asked, "Ali, what is up about Iran?"

After a short silence, I said, "Everything is ok buddy. I missed you a lot."

The he faced Jones and said, "You must be Arash, the Iranian reporter and journalist who has raised a lot of voices and reactions. It is so weird that I see you here."

Jones said, "They usually send such reporters and journalists abroad not to make a lot of noise."

The prodigy said, "It is better to have a rest now. Then I take you out to walk in New York. As I told you before I take you to the New York museum and my friend and I help you for making your documentary."

Then he stretched his finger on his lips as the sign of "zipping your mouth". He took us towards the bathroom. He stood in the tub and closed the bath curtain. We stood by the tub in an area about two square meters. He stuck a piece of paper on the wall. On the top of the paper, it was written, "We are looking for a team which buys virus. This virus is like the virus of influenza but more fatal. For curing the disease, each person must spend about one hundred dollar to buy the anti-virus drug. The afflicted person must use the drug and the disease cannot be cured by resting and right nutrition. In case the afflicted person doesn't use the drug, the disease will remain and the afflicted person might die due to physical weakness."

I wrote on a piece of paper, "Buyer? Seller?"

He wrote, "One seller and ten buyers. Some governments' delegations. A bid."

Jones wrote, "The price? How and where?"

He wrote, "Twenty billion dollars. Easily contagious through shaking hands, kissing and touching substances. We don't know the distributer yet. The main issues are making it, buying it and distributing it."

I wrote, "Do we kill the seller and rob the drug? Is that all?"

The prodigy fisted on his palm and wrote, "No, if we rob the drug, the producer makes it again and give it to a seller."

Jones wrote, "Is it here or somewhere else?"

The prodigy wrote, "It is definitely here in New York. But the main issue is the buyers; ten buyers from ten countries. Each buyer can purchase up to twenty billion dollars online so we must pocket something about two hundred billion dollars."

I didn't like the last word that he wrote. Were we going to do the mission for money or protecting people? I wished I could write them but I knew it would be useless as he wouldn't answer me.

Of course we goanna fix up the maker too but first the sellers and the buyers. To perform our big world plan, first we need a lot of money and second we must identify those bastards. Tony fisted on the prodigy's chest, removed the paper from the wall and crumpled it. Then by pointing to his lips, he notified him to zip his mouth which meant, in fact, not to write anymore.

The prodigy held his hands up when he got that he made a mistake. Jones shook his head. I was looking at them and thinking about this issue that we had to have a lot of money and identify those bastards in order to perform that big world plan. Perform that big world plan? What plan? I was ignorant about Bin Laden mission. It could be something more important than Bin Laden's mission that caused Tony to have such a reaction and the prodigy to close his mouth.

He stuck another big piece of paper on the wall. He wrote, "Ali, Arash and I...bid...buyers...representative...all unknown...picture...finding the head...bid with presence of both sides...all representatives just are seen once at the bid and then will be killed. A five-member team for tracing each buyer."

I wrote, "The time and the place of the bid?"

He wrote, "Not clear yet."

He removed the paper and stuck another one on which it was written, "As soon as the governments' delegations enter New York within the next two or three days, the bid will be held ultimately five days later. I am announcing it right now because the bid might be held sooner than the time we expect and some countries might be left from it. One hundred people accompany us in this plan; fifty people in the operative team and fifty people in the informative team besides four of us."

He wrote on the bottom of the page, "No question or answer."

Then he removed the paper. Jones and Tony left the bathroom and then left the flat. I was fed up with being played like a wind-up doll and I wanted to do what I had in mind but at the appropriate time. When they don't answer your questions, you must do something that makes them come and answer even the questions which you haven't posed yet. I wanted to do so but I had to wait. My mind was entangled with issues like "how did I know that their previous answers were true and why did I have to trust them"? Although they saved my life but it might just be a part of their play as they were good actors. One of the worst things that might happen in your life is that you can't trust anyone and anything.

It was ten at night and the hotel servant kicked on the door and brought coffee.

Jones said, "We didn't order coffee."

The servant smiled and said, "Someone ordered it for you and he said that it was an order by the cowboy."

I nodded and the servant left the room. Jones went towards his bag and took a spray out of it. He picked up the tray of the cups of coffee. He sprayed the back of the tray. A statement appeared. Behind the hotel at ten thirty. Not soon or late. The main party.

We packed what we needed and were behind the hotel on time. An Audi stopped in front of us. The windows were dark and the driver couldn't be seen. The window came down a bit and a half burnt cigar was thrown out. Jones went towards the car and opened the back door. He sat and said, "Come on."

I sat in the car. I thought Tony was in the car but it was the prodigy. Jones asked, "Are you our driver tonight?"

The prodigy said, "No, I am your boss tonight. You don't need to talk in secret words and you can say everything you like in this car."

I said, "Tell us about the plan."

He said, "I am the representative of one of the virus buyers and you both are my bodyguards. The session will be held in an underground city."

Jones said two times, "Underground city ... underground city ..."

The prodigy said, "The name isn't underground city; the name is dream city. The underground dream city, exactly underground."

I repeated like Jones in my mind, "Underground city ... underground city."

I didn't have any imaginary image of what was said. The prodigy looked at me through the front mirror but he didn't say anything. He drove to the city suburb and stopped the car in a desolate street. He turned back to us and said, "Listen to me carefully. That is an underground city. A city under the ground. Do you understand? A city like the other cities on the ground. The difference is that it isn't on the ground; it is under the ground. It might be at the size of a small town but its name is the underground city. The underground dream city. The people who live in this city will stay there forever and aren't permitted to exit it. The most important gatherings of the world are held in this city. The issue that why there must be such a city, I will talk about it later. The underground city is the best place of the world from the view point of security. That is why the auctions like virus bid are held in there in order not to be robed if it is betrayed. So a buyer is led to the venue in best security condition. An inspection is also done in there attentively. In the inspection, your eyes, finger print and DNA will be inspected attentively and you will be killed in case there is the slightest doubt about you; especially you two who are dead in fact."

I grinned and asked, "Well, so are we going to die in there?"

The prodigy said, "Look, don't worry. While you were in anesthesia, we made some changes in your retina, finger tissue and DNA. You aren't David Darbont no more by changing them. It is the same for Jones. So don't worry."

I gazed at his eyes. He had no right to do that. Who let him do that? That was my own body. It was right that he saved my life but he had no right to do that. The prodigy noticed how I was looking at him.

He said, "Look David, I know that you want to cut off my head from the neck right now but once I will explain you everything; please just help right now."

I liked to continue the play on my own wishes. I liked to leave them high and dry at the time of going to the underground city or to threaten them to answer all my questions. I might also kill both of them. I had no reason for killing them but Sara's death could be an excuse for killing. Sara died while they were trying to rescue us. If they hadn't helped, we would have been killed that night by the mercenaries. I had no choice. I had to wait more.

I thought of myself, "The underground city; what type of city it might be."

I had nothing to lose so it was better to continue the play. Killing them took me to nowhere. Being with them was safe but how did I know that I wouldn't be killed like the other representatives and bodyguards after the bid?

The prodigy told us things about the city atmosphere. It was about half an hour that we were riding in a dark solid desert with no path and we were all speechless. The prodigy stopped and switched off the car. We were in a desolate dessert in which there was nothing.

A robot's voice was heard from the car speaker.

"Introduce yourself."

The prodigy said, "The representative...thirty six...passing code, 3232632."

The car started to move without the prodigy's control on the steering wheel or the gas pedal. The car was moving and went to each direction as it wished. After some minutes riding in a barren area which had no view to nowhere, the car ran on a slope direction and all of a sudden the city lights allured our eyes. It was really an underground city and we were able to see the whole city from where the car was placed. It was a city with a high ceiling which embraced numerous high-rises. The car moved again after a short stop and we rode about one kilometer to reach the suburb of the city. The car was still controlled. We entered a street. The city had everything, casino, coffee shop, hotel, restaurant, club and whatsoever is usually found in a city. They were full of customers and people were busy in there. It was exactly as if you went from one city to another. But what would you think if you saw such a city, no matter how small, with such facilitates under the ground? What would you take it for but a dream? It was my fault that didn't take the film, "Truman Show" as a real story. We must take the films, stories and theatres serious. The films, stories and theatres are today's imaginations which come true tomorrow. Many films are produced to prepare the addressee's mind like many films and soap operas which were made to prepare minds for accepting a black president. A black president. The American people think they have a choice in election but the psychological play of the government is so strong that don't let anyone have a right choice. They work on people's mind with a pre-planned program that lead people to choose what the government wants.

Although it has a ceiling but a fabricated sun might also rise every morning like the one that was in "Truman Show". Of course it was night and there was no star or moon in the sky but the city was shining by the lights of the city.

I was thinking of myself, "Do the people in the city know where they are? Do they know that there is another world? They might also be born in here and they think it is the whole world."

We reached the end of a street in which there was the highest building of the city. The building was so high that reached the ceiling.

The car stopped and the robot's voice was heard again from the car speaker.

"Entrance code."

The prodigy said, "The representative...thirty six...passing code, 3232632."

The voice said, "The second code."

The prodigy said, "3232555B."

The voice said, "The third code."

The prodigy said, 3232666C.

The entrance door was opened and the automatic car entered. It was a big, clean and light parking lot. The car went towards the end of the parking lot and was placed in the car lift. The lift moved up. I knew it was a thirty two-store building as I counted them before the entrance. The lift reached the thirty second floor but it didn't stop. The tip of that building couldn't pass through the ground so it might be in the heart of a mountain. The lift stopped and the car moved into a dark corridor. It turned many times until it reached a place whose end was light. We entered another parking lot. The other cars entered from the other corridors and stopped somewhere.

The voice said, "You are welcome. You can get out. Our friends guide you towards the gathering place."

We got out of the car. There were some doors in front of us. Two agents guided us towards one of the doors. The whole corridor was white; the floor, the wall and even the ceiling. About twenty meters ahead, there were two agents with a device beside them. When we reached them, one of them said, "Hand over your guns."

We did as they said.

The second agent said, "Please stand in front of the device and look at the opposite sensor. Put all your ten fingers on the screen in front of your chest. A needle enters your right arm which isn't too much painful. Then I announce that you can go after the test is over."

Once again I believed that the prodigy was really a prodigy. I could be identified by none of them, not eye, not finger print and not DNA. But I was still furious with him that he did that to me. We passed through the identification gate. All corridors were ended into a big salon. In the end of the salon, there was a big door which was opened into another big salon. We entered the gathering salon.

The agent in front of the door said, "The representative must sit on the seat number nine. The bodyguards must sit on the seats number sixty six and sixty seven."

We went and sat. I was checking the size of the entrance door, exit door, the height of the wall, the material of the floor, dimensions of the salon and the other things. Ten chairs were in front of the tribune for the representatives and the bodyguards' chairs were placed some meters further behind them. There were some cases within the salon which took my attention. All bodyguards like Jones and I were bald and wearing black glasses. And the more interesting case was that there were some female bodyguards who were bald and wearing black glasses too. Despite their heads didn't have the slightest movement but I knew that their eyes were cautious enough.

But the representatives were sitting beside each other with usual clothes on their assigned seats. The gathering salon's lights were turned off and the platform's lights were turned on. Someone appeared by coming through the curtains. He had makeup like the Joker in the film, "Dark Knight". He stood by the microphone and said, "Ladies and gentlemen! Welcome! I hope the long way wouldn't make you tired. Anyway such a long way is just for protecting you. You are in the underground dream city right now, a city with about 99/99 percent security. No radio waves, TV waves or internet networks work in here. So don't check your mobiles for midnight love messages."

Some representatives burst into laughter.

Joker cleared his voice and said, "People in this city enjoy entire health and have been kept aloof from any type of illness or threat. Here is, in fact, that very utopia which we are about to make for people and we will provide some governments with the technology of building such a city...please pay attention, just some governments."

The representatives clapped and the Joker continued, "But today...why have we gathered in here? For a big bid. Maybe the biggest bid of the history. A bid with the basic recommended price of twenty billion dollars. The huge monitor behind me has been divided into ten sections for each dear representative present in here."

The monitor with ten sections was turned on.

The Joker continued, "Before starting the auction, you can enter your secret codes in the monitors which are placed in front of you to connect the relative bank. As soon as we reach a conclusion, the money in your account will be transferred into ours and our tonight production will be given to the winner. Any question?"

A representative raised his hand. The joker pointed at him and said, "Yes, please."

The representative asked, "Twenty billion dollars is a huge amount of money. I or maybe all of us who are present in here want to know how you guarantee that your production will bring us in return the same money along with the interest."

The Joker said, "Well, it is a good question. I explain it for you with a simple calculation. This production, 500 cc in weight, can afflict fifty thousand people at first stage and with regard to people communications within the big and busy cities; this number can increase to two hundred and fifty thousand during six hours. After one day, it reaches one million. After two days, three millions. After four days, six millions. Now reckon how many after one month. A virus can stay alive just some hours out of a man's body but this virus can stay alive about forty hours out of a man's body and about six mounts inside a man's body while it remains transferable. By a progressive calculation, it will be able to afflict one billion people within one month. Now multiply this number with one hundred dollars; the resulted amount will be the money you will gain by selling the medicine of the virus."

Another representative asked, "If it can bring such a huge income, why don't the producer profit it?"

All representatives said, "Ohhhhh."

"It was exactly my question too. If such a thing has been made and can bring such an income, why should they sell it and skip the huge income?"

The Joker put his fingers on his mouth. He grinned and said, "Oh my God! It seems some friends in here don't know the rules of the play. Of course you are right. You are just the representatives. The producer is just the producer, the seller is just the seller and the buyer is just the buyer. If someone goes beyond its authorities..."

A representative stood up and said in Arabic accent, "I buy."

The Joker smiled and said, "It is excellent. It seems our auction has been started."

A credit of twenty billion dollars was appeared on the ten-section monitor.

The Joker said, "Ok so we start. Twenty billion dollars, one...twenty billion, two... twenty one billion... twenty one billion...now twenty two billion...what? I didn't hear well...a bit louder...yes, I heard it now. Oh my God! Thirty billion dollars...thirty billion dollars, one... thirty billion dollars, two...no more? No more?...No more? Thirty one billion...thirty one billion... thirty one billion, one...thirty one billion, two..."

The silence prevailed over the salon. The Joker smashed the hammer on the table and said, "Thirty one billion, three and over...over...over."

All of a sudden all credits changed into zero on the monitor. The Joker's face appeared on it and a robotic voice said, "Sorry for stealing your money, hahaha."

The cacophonous robotic voice was so high that all representatives put their hands over their ears but the bodyguards still sat with no move. The Joker's face also seemed agitated.

The representatives looked at each other. An uproar rose. The bodyguards all were standing with no moving and talking. The rep number one stood up and two bodyguards after him. The rep number two stood up and two bodyguards after him. All representatives were nervous and raised their voice loudly in different languages and got out of the salon. The prodigy got up. Jones and I accompanied him. We got out of the salon. The car stopped in front of us and we got in. It was still the automatic car.

Jones asked, "What was wrong? It seemed something bad happened."

The prodigy looked at Jones and then looked at me. Then he guffawed loudly. He was out of breath by guffawing. He gasped and then guffawed again.

While he was laughing, he said, "Two hundred... two hundred billion...we pocketed two hundred billion... two hundred billion dollars...who believes that? It was the biggest fraudulence of the history."

He got stomachache out of laughing and started to message it.

I asked, "Two hundred billion dollars? Is it possible so easily?"

The prodigy stopped laughing promptly. He looked at me and said, "Hey, look around. Was it so easy? How many years of planning have been behind this work? Look! You know, you are also like the other ones who just only see. A weightlifter comes to a platform and lifts a very heavy weight within some seconds and becomes a champion. Then we say he easily lifted the weight and got gold. It is good that the weightlifter doesn't hear those words because he might die by depression. But you said those words exactly in front of the weightlifter of this event and I must confess that you make me sick."

It was the first time that the prodigy got furious against me. I looked around and found that the car was moving on the ground. The moonlight lit everywhere. The car was turned off automatically. The prodigy started the car and got the control of the car. When we took distance from the city, I noticed the other cars which moved towards the highway too. They were stopped but we were going ahead.

I said," I think something is happening."

The prodigy said, "They are going to hell one by one."

The prodigy pressed a button and said, "From zero to all operative teams...did you receive my sent images? You must have received them so far."

A voice said, "Yes sir, we received just right now and we are reviewing them."

The prodigy said, "I am talking to all operative teams. Report your positions."

"Number one, Car exploded, no more tracing."

"Number two, Car exploded, no more tracing."

"Number three, Car exploded, no more tracing."

"Number four, Car exploded, no more tracing."

"Number five, Car exploded, no more tracing."

"Number six, Car exploded, no more tracing."

"Number seven, Car exploded, no more tracing."

"Number eight was stopped."

The prodigy murmured to himself, "We are number nine."

"Number ten was stopped."

The prodigy fisted on the steering wheel. No more voice was heard. We waited for some minutes.

"Number ten is speaking...the representative number ten's car which was stopped, moved again."

The prodigy said, "Chase it carefully. To all groups, keep the cars under surveillance; even they have been exploded."

We were on the highway that another message came.

"Unfortunately we can't chase it more. The car was transferred into a helicopter and it is on flight now."

The prodigy said, "Don't worry." Then he continued, "From zero to the backing headquarter number ten. Trace it by satellite."

"Your message was received. The helicopter is under surveillance."

"Number eight is speaking. The car moved. It was transferred into a helicopter and it is on flight now."

Another voice said, "The helicopter is under surveillance."

I felt that the prodigy was agitated and couldn't analyze the events. The play was too complicated that I couldn't have the slightest analysis. The prodigy was nervous and agitated. For the first time I saw that sweat broke out his temples.

The sun was rising in the sky. We were all speechless. I remembered the first sunrise with Sara. We stayed in the mountains all night until to see, as Sara said, the most beautiful sunrise of the world. Sara called me, "Wake up my love...wake up, I want to show you the most beautiful sunrise of the world." I woke up and went out of the tent.

There was no sunrise yet. We sat on a rock facing the east. She put her head on my shoulder and we were looking at the horizon while it was going to get light little by little. The horizon was changing to orange and pink and as it was getting lighter, Sara was breathing deeper and faster. As it was getting light, the first sun rays abruptly burst out at us. Sara took my hands between his hands and pressed them on her chest.

I asked," Why do you think it is the most beautiful sunrise of the world?"

She answered, "Because my head is on your shoulder and your hands are on my chest."

I looked at it again. It was the most beautiful sunrise of the world.

Weird sounds came from the car's speakers which got me out of my remembrances. The prodigy listened to the sounds more attentively and then said, "Over."

He turned off all sending and receiving devices in the car. He gulped down his saliva. Then he cleared out the sweat of his forehead and temples and said, "I hope we haven't been betrayed."

I asked, "What is wrong?"

He said, "The sound that came from the speaker was like the sound of a tracer. These sounds are usually produced when the transmitting waves are traced."

Then he asked, "What do you think about the underground city?"

I said, "It was unbelievable. It was just like a dream."

What about you Jones; what do you think?

Jones said, "Despite of seeing with my own eyes but it isn't believable yet."

We were on our way to New York to come back to the hotel. I missed the city. I missed walking at the busy Times Square and watching a performance with Sara. I wished I could still go to the Metropolitan Art Museum with Sara and she could, like a guide, explain enthusiastically about the statues and paintings in there. I wished...but Sara was no more with me and New York with its all beauty was of no significance to me. After all those events, I was like a prisoner who went from one house to another without having permission for recreation. We waited for some hours. It was a dead silence and if you wanted to talk, you had to write. Tony along with two more guys entered. It was the first time that I saw new guys except the other members of our group. They were both muscular like me. One of them was like hippies with long hair and beard and the other one was like a trucker with a cap.

We were silent. We entered the bathroom. This time six people. The hippy stood in the tub and the rest of us stood in front of the tub. We closed the curtain. The hippy wrote on a piece of paper, "Seven teams, killed off. We, one team.

Two teams are left. One team, the Iranian agent. One team, the Qatari agent. Thirty-one billion, Iranians. A question, why hasn't the Qatari team been killed off?"

The prodigy wrote, "Is there any connection between the two teams? Where does the virus break out?"

He wrote, "Negative". Then he shook his head out of sorrow.

Tony picked up the marker to write something but he changed his mind.

The prodigy wrote, "Two teams under surveillance. Over."

We got out of the bathroom. We all sweated. Those two guys left us. Tony and the prodigy were absorbed in thinking. They sat at a table, wrote something on a piece of paper and showed at each other.

Suddenly I got up and said, "I want to go."

They gazed at me.

Tony asked, "Hey ape, what a hell do you want to go?"

I said, "Everywhere except here and with everyone except you all."

The prodigy looked at the ceiling.

Tony said, "We thought we can count on you."

I said, "You counted on me for many things without my permission."

I pointed at my eyes, fingers and passport.

Jones said, "Hey buddy, all those trouble was for you. We could let them..."

I said, "Ok, why didn't you let them?"

Tony said, "Look! We committed a big mistake and we don't know what we must do now."

Jones said, "Hey buddy, we saw humanitarianism in your soul. Many people see many wrongdoings but remain silent out of fear or they are bought by money to shut up but you followed none of those dirty ways; you were after truth."

I said, "I was but it seems I am not supposed to find the truth. I am like a doll in your hands and you behave me as you wish. Please finish with it. I want to leave you. Do you let me go or do you want to kill me that I don't care about it."

Tony and Jones looked at the prodigy who was still looking at the ceiling. They were waiting for him to say something and he finally said, "look! I like to help you to make your documentary but I am not sure about you. You say you want to go and it confirms my distrust towards you. It isn't clear if you want to stay and make your documentary or not. I don't like to toil over a case and then you go and do your own business."

I pointed to myself and said, "You are ruining my documentary. I don't know why..."

I became silent and wrote on a piece of paper, "Dagellas Cliff". Then I continued, "I was afflicted with so many misfortunes. I don't understand your plans and the events which occur. I am bored of all these. I must make my own documentary but you are after greater filmmakers and don't care the filmmakers like me."

The prodigy said, "Look! You don't know how valuable it was what you did tonight."

I said, "I am happy for that but it doesn't change my decision. What about my documentary?"

The prodigy wrote, "What would you do if I say just some steps are left to reach the head of the T2 operation?"

By seeing that statement, I blew a fuse. The scene of how Sara was killed came in front of my eyes. I was gasping severely. They all three were looking at me and waited for my answer. Now as I planned it before I was able to put them into trouble. The prodigy revealed his ace card but you can devalue an ace card when it seems of no importance.

I said," I make my documentary, with or without you."

Jones wrote, "What is your aim in this world? Just killing the head of the T2 operation? And then he wrote, "Hey buddy, do you think you have no more duty in this world?"

I asked, "For example what?"

The prodigy wrote, "To stop killing millions of people. We have gathered here to save people's lives." Then he said, "Ali, you are a professional filmmaker and reporter. You can make many good films for removing misfortune and plight from the earth. It isn't something small. You can make many films by the cooperation of our machinery."

It was difficult to write what my heart said but there was no choice but to write them, "The United Nations' words were also on the behalf of people. Despite of all its power and authorities, ten million people have at least been killed so far and ten million more have also died out of hunger and poverty."

I continued, "Let's count the number of people who have died by their negligence; it might be more than the number of people who died in Second World War."

The prodigy wrote, "So why did you become the UN soldier?"

His question was like a bullet that disintegrated my head. I gazed at his eyes and said, "I had a dream too – a dream that was passing the same direction."

Tony said, "Hey ape, tell us about your dream."

I said, "My dream makes you laugh as your plans do the same for me."

Jones said, "Please Ali, tell us about your dreams, please. It has been a lot of years that I know you and I know what those dreams are and what type of films you are interested to make but Tony and the prodigy don't know about them."

I took a deep breath and said, "My dream was that I wanted to be a good director in there and I had good ideas for making film which could save people's lives; the films which could be made during all those years by the company but it didn't make them."

I was silent for a moment and then I said, "Now all my dreams have died."

Tony said, "We are able to bring those dreams back to you and help you to make them buddy."

I grinned and asked, "You mean I come back there?"

Tony said, "No ape! It means stay with us. Our machinery is becoming bigger and bigger little by little." Then he wrote, "Our machinery isn't like UN which is under the domination of some bully countries. Unlike UN which bears a false name, our machinery doesn't work for just some specific governments. This machinery is for people without regarding religion, the skin color and race."

I said, "I thought I was a dreamer since I was a little child but now I see you are a better dreamer than me."

Jones said, "Hey buddy! Many of our dreams are like realities or will be like realities but what can help us to reach them is our beliefs. Why don't you want to believe us? Leave us whenever you see that we are doing something wrong which is against humanitarianism."

He pointed out the prodigy and said, "He worked hard two years for the last night film; for rescuing millions of people. Do you understand? Millions of people."

The prodigy laughed and said, "look! And you definitely remember what Tony and Arash bestowed me as a reward."

Tony said, "Shut up! You shut up! If you had told us that where the actor of the significant film was, we wouldn't have done those damn things with you. You made us to do that with you, you bastard ape."

The prodigy guffawed and said, "Look, I can't also trust you otherwise I get assured that you believe in our ideas for filmmaking. We made good films during last years. Our films are all for the whole world; you watched one or two of them. Now come here and read our idea for the new film."

He put a piece of paper on the table on which it was written, "It is supposed the virus to be broken out and the gained income will be a titanic number. What we can do now is just follow the events and we don't know who planned it. What we know is that a malignant virus has been sold. The virus was supposed to be sold to one group but it might jointly have been sold to two groups. Both groups are forces affiliated with the delegations of two countries. They entered New York. At first look, it seems we encounter just two governments but it will be clear soon how far they can expand their activity. There might likely be side countries which do anything wrong as they wish without the main countries' knowledge. Another issue is that selling of this virus to those groups seems to be a play. The income gained by selling the virus is so suggestive that cannot dissuade the capitalists of the countries like USA, England, Russia and Israel. They are rich countries and can easily invest on cases like this. They usually recommend higher prices and then withdraw. It is a play with no doubt. Now we must find the password of the play."

The prodigy's watch alarmed. He smiled and said, "Look! This is my gift to you." Then he wrote, "The key responsible piece for T2 operation." He continued, "I want to acquaint you with one of the big American film producers tonight."

******

The car set off. I was looking at the street through the car's dark windows. No more I wanted to go to a café and eat something. No more I wanted to walk in the Central Park. No more I wanted to see the Brooklyn Bridge or the Umpire State. I just wanted to see the head of the operation and take his life but I was thinking all the time what kind of killing could calm me. I thought even ripping him off couldn't calm me but would I rip him off if I found him? What about you? Just imagine. Someone has been the cause of dozens of people death and the very issue caused you to lose the most valuable individual of your life. Now what do you do? What kind of killing calms you? Do you forgive him? Really!? But it is a big folly to forgive this kind of people. You can forgive when you know what happened was just an accident and there were no intention but you cannot forgive dirty guys who shit the world with their dirty jobs.

We entered a high-rise and went into the tenth parking floor of the building. The lift door was opened and we entered a dark place in the end of which a light lamp was seen. Two people were standing there and one was sitting on a chair. My heart was beating fast. I was stepping faster. There was some smell of acid. Tony and Jones were left behind but the prodigy tried to step along with me. When I came closer, I found that the guy who was sitting on the chair was Edward, one of the senior officers of the intelligence service of the UN; one of those who just used to sit at the table and order. He was wearing suit and fright and anxiety could be observed on his face. The two guys who were standing there went away and vanished in the darkness. When they left the place, I got sure that Edward was a criminal. He tried to act calm. Just some steps were left to reach him when I stopped in front of him. First he looked at the prodigy and then looked at me. When he looked at me, his eyes opened wider but he didn't say anything. Tony also reached while limping. Jones was also with him. We were like a fire squad which was ready to shoot. Edward looked at Tony and Jones. He got up. He smiled mirthlessly, opened his arm towards Tony and said, "How are you commander? I never thought that the cunning Tony might be the planer of all those games. I appreciate for all you have done to keep me safe."

Tony gazed at his eyes and didn't bring out his hands out of his pockets.

Jones and I were standing on the right side of Tony. Tony pointed to us with a head gesture and asked, "Do you know these two guys?"

Edward looked at Jones and me and said, "Their faces are familiar to me but I don't think I can remember where I saw them."

Tony said, "But you know them very well. They can't be very unfamiliar to you with bald heads. Do you know why you are here?"

Edward said, "No...I don't know exactly...I mean...I mean I am here as a security guard...these days...these days we are so busy and the General Assembly of UN...and so on..."

He was speaking brokenly. He became speechless for a moment and then continued, "But...but I appreciate all of you for saving my life."

Tony said, "We didn't save your life. In fact we want to take your life."

Edwards gulped down his saliva and looked at all of us one by one. Then he faced Tony and said, "Do you...do you understand what you are saying? I did my best to help you to register your private organization."

Tony said, "I never forget people's aid but I can't also ignore your rascal behavior."

Edward who started gasping loosened his tie and said, "What are you talking about? I... I don't know."

Tony said, "So let me tell you about the past so as to make you understand that you cannot take us as fool guys. Ten years ago, we found that dirty jobs took place at the organization. We traced them until we reached George and he caught us red-handed but he made a big mistake. He didn't inform you of being betrayed not to be omitted from your dirty band. So they took Catherine as hostage for reaching us but the story changed and we fixed them up without leaving trail of ourselves. Then you doubted George that he might have a role in the happenings. You made troubles for him many times. You interrogated him times and times but your investigation went to nowhere. The best way for us was to keep silent to make you think everything was over and now after ten years we succeeded to trap you again."

Edward said with shaking voice, "I...I feel dizzy...I don't understand...it is all Greek to me...you want to say...you killed George? Oh my Goodness! I can't believe. Why? What is damn with you?"

Jones went forward one step and said, "The T2 operation Edward; isn't the code familiar to you?"

I could see the shaking of his hands clearly. The big drops of sweats were falling down on his face. He found that we called his bluff. He tried to act calm. Then he said, "Well!...you are in my trap...so...so you killed Daggles Cliff too!?"

Tony grinned, held his hands up and said, "Hey guys, we have been trapped; let's escape." Then he guffawed like lunatics.

Edward who was thoroughly frightened and felt groggy, lounged on the chair and loosened his tie more.

Tony said, "It is time this useless fiddle-faddle to be shut down." We ring the alarm bell for closing the organization. It doesn't matter how long it takes for us to shut it down; what is important for us is that we are decisive to do it."

Edward who was still trying to act cool guffawed and said, "You all...you all seemed be out of mind. Do you understand what you are saying? Do you really think you are able to close UN? Hahaha..."

Jones said, "I wish you could be alive when it is closed."

The laughter faded on his face. He gulped down his saliva and said. "You...you know that many generous and self-sacrificed people are serving in this organization. You...you know that they help the world poor nations not to be died out of hunger."

Tony said, "Yeah you bastard piece of nothing! We aren't usual guys like the other ones. We also know about those good guys. But if those very generous and self-sacrificed guys find that they are working under the surveillance of a couple of bastards, they would definitely do something about it. If they know that a plight like cancer afflicted the organization, they would leave the organization with no hesitation. And if they know that people like you are, in the organization, responsible for the death of millions of people, they will serve no more in the organization under the title of UN."

He yelled, "What?...what did you say?...millions of people?...I am responsible for the death of millions of people?...what are you talking about? Don't stigmatize me."

Tony said, "It seems you got very old or you think we are so dump...Rwanda...in fact Rwanda genocide...do you remember anything? You were one of those people who caused the death of two million people by preventing an on-time measure."

I could easily see that his hands was shaking and was becoming numb. It wasn't clear where he was looking at; no words or movement. I didn't want him to die out of fear. It wasn't fair that he had an easy death.

The prodigy looked at me and said, "Look, he is the head of all those barbarianism; now what are you going to do?"

I didn't move and didn't say anything. I could kill him by feasting his chest or by kicking his head. I could smash all his bones. But none of them made me calm. The image of Sara's death, the broken jaw of that young boy and that pregnant woman with the fetus on the ground were in front of my eyes. But I couldn't find no way of torturing that could satisfy my revenging appetite for all those events.

The prodigy's watch alarmed loudly and I knew that the sound meant something important.

He looked at his watch and his eyes opened wider. We all looked at him and he was staring at his watch.

Tony asked, "What happened?"

The prodigy grinned and said, "First fix up this bastard."

We were standing without any movement.

The prodigy said, "Look David, we have no time."

I didn't move or talk again.

The prodigy said, "I guessed your reaction before! Let me fix him up; I do it in a way that you make a kick out of it."

He clapped his hands and said, "Be ready buddies."

The place where those two guys were vanished in darkness became light. They were standing near a hook which was hanging from the ceiling. There was an iron valve under the hook. They came towards him.

Plea...please Tony...let me explain.

The two guys tried to push him towards the hook. He was struggling. I got near him and fisted on his mouth. He became listless. They fastened his hands and legs by rope and hanged him from the hook. The blood was stretched from the corner of his lips towards his chin. He was gazing at Tony and didn't avert his look from him. His look was full of begging.

One of those two guys opened the iron valve under the hook. The smell of acid filled the atmosphere more than before. Now he got that what they were going to do with him.

Tony... Tony...please... Tony, for the sake of the past... Tony, we are friends...Tony...

The rope was coming down little by little.

He put his feet on the edge of the two sides of the valve to prevent getting inside. I went towards him and kicked him on the stomach. His legs were set free. They reached the acid. Smoke was raised from his shoes and when his feet reached the acid, he started sobbing. He was continuously struggling but the more he was struggling the more he was immerging into acid. When he immerged down until his waist, there was no more weeping and didn't breathe no more. The prodigy gestured them to release the rope and they released it. He sank in the acid.

We got out of the building. It was hot but I was shivering. The sweat broke out all my body.

When we got into the car, Tony asked, "Well ape, what's up?"

The prodigy said, "The location of breaking out the virus has been assigned."

Jones asked, "Well, where is it?"

The prodigy said, "Mecca."

Episode Four

We were sitting in a restaurant in Mecca. It was the Arabic Zil-Hajj month and Muslims entered the city in mass from different countries to perform the annual pilgrimage ceremony. The hotels were full or they were going to be full. We went to a hotel which wasn't as busy as the other ones and the people in there were different, both passengers and the staff. All passengers had food in their own rooms and the restaurant was empty. We also ate food in our room. But once, the prodigy asked us to eat in the restaurant. When we sat in the restaurant, the other passengers entered it little by little and the restaurant which wasn't usually seen with not more than ten people, now it had been stuffed with passengers. Nothing was normal. I smelled gunpowder from their clothes when they passed by me which meant that they were all equipped with guns. None of them ordered food and they just sat in there without talking. Jones and I were sitting at a table with various foods in front of us. We had no appetite for eating and we were just playing with the food. It was in fact an excuse for us to spend time somehow. I chased every movement in there and I was thinking about the issue that what would be better to do if we got into a scuffle so I was reviewing different scenes of conflicts in my mind.

Tony and the prodigy also joined us. Tony was gasping and limping as usual. They came and sat at the table. I easily found that all people in there were security forces and their nationalities could also been recognized by their features – English, American, Israeli, Swedish, Japanese, Chinese, French Russian and German.

All of a sudden all heads were turned towards the entrance door of the restaurant and I turned my head either.

A man and a woman entered the restaurant that allured all looks. He was a bulky broad-shouldered man. He was taller than two meters. His suit, shirt, belt and even his shoes were white. He was a White with light hair and eyes. The woman with him was a bit shorter than him. She was broad-shouldered too with a long black dress and shawl. Her eyes were completely black as if they had no white part. They looked around and came towards us with slow steps. They got near and stopped. The man looked at the prodigy and shouted loudly as if he wanted everyone there to hear what he was going to say, "Is the Phoenix with you?"

Suddenly all people in the restaurant got up and went towards the exit door. They were all frightened while they were leaving that place and I could see fear on each and every man or woman's face.

The prodigy told them to sit. They sat. The prodigy pointed at the man and said, "Zal."

Then he pointed at the woman and said, "Roudabeh."

The woman smiled and nodded.

Zal said, "We are duty-bound to be at your service to the best of our ability but talking straight, if something goes against people, there would be no support."

The prodigy said, "Nothing must be in the direction of hurting people and if it had been like this, we wouldn't have been here now and asked for help."

The woman said, "The Iranian agent went to hell in the procedure of the auction but the Qatari agent who is himself a foreign influencer in that country is still alive and kicking but the Qatari agents don't enjoy the ability as well as the motivation for playing such a big ruthless game. We must find or you must find the guy who supports this Arab sheikh."

Zal said, "And we know that you found it or are going to find it and our condition for cooperation is that inform us if you found it or are going to find it.

The prodigy fisted his palm a couple of times and pressed his lips. Then he said, "What do we receive in return?"

Zal gazed at the prodigy and narrowed his eyes but didn't say anything.

The prodigy continued, "I think nothing we receive in return. Is it right?"

Roudabeh said, "We are supporting you and regard it as a big job. Saudi Arabia isn't where you can easily bring your forces and do something so you need us to help you. No country supports you but our forces are all around Saudi Arabia. All countries are aware of the virus but even Saudi Arabia refused to stop this year's hajj ceremony and announced that everything is under control but we know that this country is not able repel such an event."

The prodigy said, "Look, all you said is right but we can easily leave this country and you get bewildered what to do. Then a catastrophe takes place and the whole world must be indemnified for the other's wrongdoing. To stop the distribution of the virus, we must receive something; a considerable amount which makes us satisfied to co-operate with you."

Zal closed his eyes.

The prodigy continued, "Look, that will be your country which will be proud of herself for the operation and it will be regarded as an honor for your country. We are helping you to gain a global honor and there will be no name of us for doing such a thing so we are expecting a good offer from you."

She boasted of herself by moving her head and said, "The Iranian nation has achieved numerous honors within history of humanity and the countries which have formed during the recent two or three centuries, feel thirsty for her blood."

The prodigy said, "So it might be good she adds another honor to the others. I think it has been a long time that it took aloof from such honors."

Zal and Roudabeh got up together. Zal said, "Wait for our final answer."

They got out of the restaurant. I took a deep breath. I felt that I kept my breath for some minutes. Tony and the prodigy were smiling. Jones and I were astonished. I smelled blood. I tuned my head towards the exit door and stared at it.

Jones asked, "What happened, David? Say something."

I said, "Here isn't safe. The smell of blood tells me that somewhere near here must be a slaughterhouse."

The prodigy was gazing at me.

Jones said, "We must leave here as soon as possible."

We got up and went towards the exit door of the hotel. I was moving ahead with my hand on my Colt under my coat. I looked outside with caution. A car turned fast on the head of the street and went away. I looked at the other side. The clean and empty street in front of the hotel became a slaughterhouse.

Slaughtered bodies were spread around – arm, leg, head. Blood was dropping down the walls and the parked cars' windows. There was no living soul in there. The prodigy came after me and stood there with no reaction while he was looking at the whole street. Tony, Jones and I were looking around. It was definitely a fight by cold weapons that made no noise. But why? The prodigy took out his glasses out of his pocket and wore them.

We moved towards the car and got into it. We went to another hotel for resting. I lay on bed and fell into asleep. Sara came to my dream. She was smiling. I was on the ground and moments later I found myself on the top of the mountains. Sara came near and was pointing at the sunrise with her finger. I looked at the sunrise. It was too red. I looked at Sara. Red tears were running from her eyes. I cleared out her tears and hugged her. I was hugging her tightly with all my strength in order to feel her soul. But my efforts for hugging her were futile and it was like that I was hugging the air. Then her head was ripped off, her legs were cut and blood was splashed to my face with whooshing sound.

A hand shook me and I was jolted awake. It was Jones. He said, "Hey, buddy, I think you had a bad dream."

I sat on the bed. I had a headache and my eyes were going to get out of their place.

I asked Jones, "Who did the slaughtering in front of the hotel?"

Jones said, "This is Zal and Roudabeh's method of slaughtering. But what happened? We don't know."

I asked, "Are Zal and Roudabeh alive?"

"I don't know."

"Where are Tony and the prodigy?"

"I don't know again."

"Well, if you know, tell me at least what are we supposed to do?"

Suddenly a sound came out of the prodigy's sack in the corner of the room. Jones jumped out of his place and went towards the closet in which we hided the guns. I also got up and took the machine gun and the Colt. We put the hands-frees in our ears.

Jones asked, "What happened?"

Tony said, "Black Water, roof, safe."

Jones opened the door and had a look inside the lobby of the hotel. He signed me to move. We entered the lobby. There was a flight of stairs in the middle of the lobby and a lift near it. I looked down the stairs. Some people were coming up. I gestured Tony to move up. When we reached two or three floors upper, I looked down again. They entered our floor and then there was the sound of smashing a door and the fire of a gun machine. We reached the thirtieth floor and then the roof. We went to the roof. There were two parachute bags on the corner of the roof for escaping. We ran towards the bags when a helicopter came up towards the roof. There were two snipers in the helicopter who shot us as soon as they saw us. Jones hided and I leaped over onto the floor. The wind force shook the helicopter out of balance and made them unable to aim us right. The helicopter took a distance from us to turn round and come back again. I looked at Jones. The roof door got opened by a kick and someone came out. I aimed his head with my Colt. The second one was going to put his leg outside but he got repentant and went inside. I signed Jones to watch over the roof door. The helicopter turned back. I got two Uzi gun machines out of my neck and aimed at the helicopter. I was at the snipers' aiming direction right now. When they saw me that I was aiming them, they withdrew backwards. I shot recklessly. First I shot inside the helicopter to scare them to look out and then I shot the main propeller and the rare propeller of the helicopter. The helicopter flew away with smoking. Jones was shooting at the roof door on and off to avoid people to come out. There was a silence for a moment and then the sound of shooting was heard from inside. First I thought it might be Tony who came to help us. We both aimed at the roof door but I was watching over my back too for the helicopter or probable attack from the opposite buildings. A howl was heard. The roof door was opened and one of the Water Black forces was thrown out. His neck was broken and one of his hands was separated. There was still the sound of skirmishing and fighting in there. Again another corpse without head was thrown out onto the roof and the sound of shooting was stopped. Another helicopter was approaching. The roof door got completely opened and Zal appeared in the entrance door. He bent down his neck and turned round his body to pass the same door through which we had passed easily. He was holding a head by hair in one hand and a Colt in the other hand. He was standing in the middle of the roof with white clothes which was soaked with blood and was shooting the helicopter which was approaching. The helicopter turned round fast and went away. The hotel alarm bell sound was raised. The police force would surely surround that place within some seconds. Zal signed us to enter the building. We went to the thirtieth floor by the stairs. People had left the rooms soon before. The alarm bell was cut. Everywhere was calm and silent. Like a slaughterhouse, the hotel's lobby was full of ripped off corpses who were Water Black forces.

We reached the end of the lobby. Zal knocked on the door with code. The door was opened. We entered. Roudabeh was sitting on the chair in the corner and was studying a book. She got up as soon as she saw Zal. She smiled and said, "Oh my dear, you messed your clothes again."

Zal smiled and said, "But you are not supposed to clean them."

She came towards Zal and hugged him in those dirty clothes.

The police forces entered the lobby and their noises could be heard. Jones and I were in full alert.

Roudabeh looked at us and said, "It is over. Make yourself at home. Nobody come to this room."

She took off his clothes and put them in a basket. I got a kick out of watching Zal's naked well-built body with a feature of about fifty five and Roudabeh's romantic reactions was also alluring to me. We noticed the wound on Zal's arm whose blood was congealed but it was open about a couple of centimeters. Roudabeh was going to cry as soon as she saw the scission on his arm and said, "Oh my dear."

Then she put her lips on his wound.

Zal said, "Your kisses can relieve the pain but can't treat the wound."

She helped Zal to sit on a table. Then she went to the bedroom and came back with a small bag.

Zal had a cigar in the corner of his lips. He picked up Roudabeh's book and started to turn over the pages. Roudabeh opened the bag and spread the aid kit tools on the table.

She looked at Zal and asked, "My dear, do you think Shahnameh's Zal was also smoking?"

Zal said, "I don't know but I know that Roudabeh wasn't nagging."

Roudabeh smiled and rolled her eyes. Then she started to stitch the wound of his arm with special needle and stitch without using local anesthesia injection. I was looking at Zal's face that didn't have the slightest facial expression change as needle pierced his arm and he was busy with smoking and reading the book.

I sat right in there behind the door and remembered Sara. Once she came back from climbing and entered the house. I noticed that she bandaged her ankle and was limping. Her facial expression indicated that she was suffering a severe pain. I went towards her.

"What happened Sara?"

"I fell down."

"You are a professional climber; how did you fall down?"

She looked at me. She was on the verge of crying. She pressed his head on my chest and said, "I don't know."

Her body's sweating smell was so sharp.

She asked, "Do you want to know why I fell down."

I nodded and said, "Tell me if you like."

She smiled and her tears ran.

She said, "I was thinking about a day that you weren't in my life...then I became absentminded, slipped over on a rock and fell down."

I burst into laughing and was guffawing loudly and incessantly. She got angry. She got up and started to beat me with her small fists. Then she got a cushion and smashed it to my head and face. She was gasping. I took her hand and seized her in my arms. She couldn't move anymore. She was still crying with smile on her lips.

I said, "Let's promise each other."

She asked, "What is that promise?"

I said, "Let's promise to continue living in each other's absence. Living alone will be definitely difficult but it is life. Let's value the moments we are together."

Someone knocked on the door with code. I got out of my dreams and jumped out of my place. We aimed our guns at the door. Roudabeh had finished with stitching and went towards her tablet and checked it. Then she clicked on the monitor with her finger and said, "Friends."

The door was opened. Tony and the prodigy entered. The prodigy went towards Zal and asked, "Hey, How are you man?"

Zal said, "I am fine when I am with Roudabeh."

Roudabeh smiled and Tony looked at me and asked, "Are you ok, ape?"

I said, "I feel better now that I see you and the prodigy."

Tony guffawed and said, "Heyyy, it seems we are getting good friends."

I nodded. The prodigy looked so alive a kicking. He sat on the chair in front of Zal. Zal gave his half smoked cigar to Roudabeh. She put it off and threw it into the garbage basket. Zal asked, "The result?"

The prodigy said, "We could just mange to prevent the breakout of the virus among people in Mecca. If it happened, we would expect a global catastrophe."

Zal extended his arm towards the prodigy and said, "Virus."

The prodigy looked at his hand and said, "We didn't achieve to gain it."

Zal got up. His white skin turned red and fisted on the table beside him.

"Damn with you...damn with you as you can't do a job right. You just always boast of doing right jobs."

The prodigy said louder, "Can't we do a job right!? Your forces were after them and they did their job well. Your forces are so strong and professional that when Black Water's forces encountered them they jumped out of their skin. You killed the Iranian connection and we killed the

Qatari connection but none of them were the head of the virus plot. They were ordered by another resource. Now imagine what a chaos would have taken place in the world of Islam if the world had recognized the Islamic countries Iran or Qatar as the main schemer of the virus plot. Imagine what a massacre would have taken. What we found is that the virus is going to be transferred to Africa. Where are they going to commit genocide; just God knows. I provide you with the whole information to chase it."

Zal said, "So you are a fair-weather friend."

The prodigy said, "If you want, I help you but I am sure that you can do it without our help."

"And you surely want your money!?"

"I did as I promised. I promised to help you to stop the massacre of millions of people and I did it but I didn't promise to gain the virus. All security forces of the other countries in mecca found that your country did a great job and it is a peerless achievement for your country."

Zal got up. He bent over a little bit towards the prodigy and said, "Why are you telling all of the time your country; you mean Iran isn't your country anymore?"

The prodigy got up to face him to talk but his head was just up to his chest and he had to hold his head up in order to gaze at his eyes. It was an uneasy atmosphere. I was pressing the Colt in my hand and fright could be seen on

Jones's face. Tony didn't move. Some seconds passed but each second was like a minute. The prodigy's answer couldn't surely be convincing for Zal and it was better for him not to answer but the prodigy held his forefinger towards Zal and said, "You..."

Roudabeh said while smiling, "Stop with it." She looked at Zal and said, "The prodigy didn't mean something bad, my dear. Is it possible that you are from the richest culture of the world and then you claim that you don't belong to that territory?"

Then she looked at the prodigy and asked, "Am I right?"

The prodigy got down his finger. Then he sat on the chair again and said, "I have never been against my country."

Zal said, "Well-done! Say my country. You must always be proud of your country even you have been afflicted with many misfortunes times and times. The culture of this country is so great that many countries have tried to keep it unknown for many years or even centuries as it has been so rich. Fighting against our country is not for missile and nuclear bomb; it is the west's obsession against our culture. That is the truth, wise man.

The west isn't afraid of being bombarded by our bombs; it is afraid that our cultural bomb might ruin their scheme and programs although people don't maintain this culture accurately because a culture needs protection. Their other obsession is Islam. But the more they ruin the feature of

Islam, the more people in western countries convert into Islam. If Islam means massacre and barbarianism so why do many people in western countries convert into Islam permanently; especially many people from the modern countries."

As he was talking, he started to gasp and his chest was wheezing. Roudabeh went to the other room and brought an oxygen mask which was attached a small oxygen tank. She put it on his mouth and Zal took some deep breath. His broad hairy chest was moving up and down. Roudabeh took Zal's hand and helped him lie on the bed. He messaged his chest and said things in Persian.

The prodigy said in calm manner, "I know what you think about me. But...they didn't behave me right."

Zal took off the mask and said, "You acted as you wished and what you did was a black mark for the intelligence service."

The prodigy said, "But what I did was the best."

Zal said, "But you did it on your own. We counted on you. You are one of the greatest Major Generals' boys of Iran."

The prodigy said, "But it wasn't clear how did you wipe this Major General from the face of the earth?"

Zal said, "It is foolish of you that you think like this. Your father was killed by bioterrorism.

The prodigy asked, "By whom?"

Zal sat on the bed and Roudabeh put a cushion behind him. He lounged on it and said, "Your father was sent to work for Mossad by the king's order in 1977. Then the revolution took place and after it, war. Your father didn't have any plan to return but he turned back by the start of war. In fact Mossad sent him to Iran to spy in the battlefronts but your father battled in the fronts with patriotism. Then Mossad found that it was cheated but they couldn't find your father because he was trained by themselves and they never thought that a king fan might change his path."

He put the mask again on his mouth and took some deep breath then he removed it again and continued, "Your father was a hidden Amir. I had been his guard for ten years. He was peerless. He named me Zal and when I got married to Mitra, he called her Roudabeh so we became Zal and Roudabeh from that day on later. Your father had a significant responsibility in Vaja. He set up a security intelligence service named, 1986 Unit. Even me as his guard was completely ignorant about his job in the unit. No one was suspicious to him as Iran was in war at that time. The unit worked under the supervision of your father not the government. Your father set up the unit to get even with Mossad and Mossad didn't also let go of your father. I protected your father in nineteen terrorism attacks against him although he was able to protect himself in my absence. By the end of war, your father was betrayed. He was dismissed and he became a serious governmental critique but he wasn't killed by the government. He was the only one who passed the Mossad, KGB, CIA and BND courses. Two or three years after he was dismissed, they wanted to return him to Vaja but...Mossad got out of the blue."

Now he could breathe better. Roudabeh looked at three of us and said, "I don't think you have more reason to stay here. You let go of the virus and threw the ball in our court. You also received your money. What is more damn wrong with you?"

The prodigy went towards Roudabeh. He stood in front of her and said, "Look! I left my country for such a contemptuous behavior; a behavior which could make our country better if it was improved. Such behaviors lead young people to leave our country and go to the western nations and make them the best. Despite of this issue that I am under no obligation due to my country and I am regarded as a fugitive but I help you to prevent many catastrophes by giving you appropriate information otherwise you would have killed me many times so far. So don't play the roles of the myths for me."

Zal stretched his arm and took the prodigy's hand while he was lying. He removed the mask, took a deep breath and said, "Come back."

The prodigy said, "I never come back. I am always looking the way ahead and I believe in that way so much that I never look back and never come back."

Zal smiled and said, "I wish you would come back but it seems you wouldn't so let me give you a gift as a friend."

He pointed to the tablet and Roudabeh gave it to him. He opened a page and held it in front of his face.

He said, "He is the very rich Arab who you are after him. He easily brings the poor Bengali, Indian and Pakistani children to Iran by passport and visa. Some dirty guys separated their organs and he sold them to richer Arabs and he became richer and richer in this way. He is right now in Mecca. I thought you would like to get even with him. Of course I know that you were chasing him better than me and would fix him up sooner or later but I just wanted to tell you that he is in Mecca. You can take a prompt measure. Be careful, Black Water's forces are after you all over the city."

******

This time we went to a hide-out, not to a hotel. The weather in the Saudi Arabia was hot and humid and took our breath. I thought it was time to come back but it seemed it was going to be a long story. Now Tony, Jones and the prodigy had been involved in a conflict.

Tony grinned and said, "I don't go to the Sheikh's house and I don't let you go there too."

Jones said, "Hey buddy! Tony is right. This measure is an entire folly. Your biggest mistake is that you forget our great aim and you don't also regard our circumstances."

The prodigy got up and went to the window. He looked out. Tony and Jones were looking at each other. They were afraid of the decision that was going to be made by the prodigy. After the events in the hotel and coming to a hide-out, we were waiting for the prodigy to send us out of the Saudi Arabia but his decision would cause delay in the procedure. His decision was to meet someone who was responsible for some events in Iran and he didn't want to miss the opportunity now that he could find him by Zal's help. Tony's forces also left the Saudi Arabia in the wake of the virus incidents in order not to be involved in conflicts with Black Water's forces. Now it was our turn to leave the country but the prodigy's decision hindered us.

The prodigy looked at three of us and said, "Well, no problem if you don't like to accompany me but nobody can stop me."

Tony got up and went towards him in limping walks and took his collar while he was in the status of both anger and begging.

He said, "Hey ape! Why don't you understand? They might trace us and we all might be killed. Now Black Water's forces in Ihram cloth among the passengers are looking for us, then you are after a private retaliation in such a situation!?"

The prodigy said, "Tony, you are a shit."

Tony let go of his collar, looked into his eyes and said, "Me!?...am I a shit?"

Tony looked at Jones and then looked at the prodigy. While his voice and hands were shivering out of anger, he asked, "Why...why are telling me this?"

The prodigy said, "Because you are really a shit."

Tony slapped him on his face. Then he pulled his gun out of his pant stock and aimed at him. Jones and I jumped out of our places and were going to do something that Tony said, "Nobody moves. I must just find right now why he is telling me this."

The prodigy's lip was ripped by his slap. He touched it with his forefinger. Then he looked at the blood on his finger and yelled out, "Shoot me damn guy. What are you waiting for? Shoot. Kill me. Shut your eyes and don't evade doing me a favor. What are you waiting for damn guy? I say that he must be killed and you know the reason well. Thousands of children have been butchered and their organs have been sold by his order and now you are telling me I am after a private retaliation!? Look Tony, you are thinking like those guys in the United Nations. You like to do things that to be showed off but the affliction of the big catastrophes like this one is so much bigger. A bastard stinking rich Sheikh are butchering hundreds of children and making a kick out of it then you tell me I am after a private retaliation!? And then you are asking me why I called you a shit!?"

Tony's face got wet and his lips were shivering. He said, "No...no...it isn't what I said. I...I..."

Jones said, "No, buddy. It isn't what he means. We have more important jobs. It would be a different story if each one of us is killed. Swear to God, be logical."

The prodigy said, "Funnily enough I am thinking logically. Our forces all left the Saudi Arabia and there is no one whom I can give the job. I do what I must do. If I am supposed to prevent doing it due to expediency, I might lose that damn guy and then that bastard will keep on his job. Then how can I claim for humanitarianism? Answer my question and then I get out of your face and leave this country."

******

We put on thawbs and agals like Arabs. We got out of the hide-out and got into the taxi which was waiting for us. It was dark. We exited Mecca. There was a checkpoint on the city border. I touched the Colt under my cloth. The prodigy who was sitting beside the driver said, "Behave normally.

We resemble Arabs but they are after Zal and Roudabeh not us."

We reached the checkpoint. The checkpoint inspectors lit inside the car by the projectors. Two police officers got their heads into the car, looked at each of us one by one and then withdrew. They asked some questions from the driver and he answered. Then they checked his documents and they let their coworkers to open the way. A frisk was enough to betray us and then I didn't really know what would happen? We got out of the city. There were big beautiful villas on the border – the villas which indicated that their owners were opulent. There were big electrical doors, stoned buildings and beautiful shining lights...

The driver asked something in Arabic and the prodigy who was sitting by him, answered in Arabic too. I got the word, "Sheikh" in their talks. The driver looked at the prodigy with astonishment and said more things in Arabic. Then he looked at the prodigy with uttering statements which seemed to be questions but he didn't answer.

The driver was yakking for two or three minutes and the prodigy said something that made him dump and he didn't talk no more.

We entered a street and the driver stopped the car in front of a house. The prodigy gave the driver some notes and they talked again in Arabic. It was more like an argument.

The prodigy gave him more notes and we got out of the car but Tony stayed inside the car.

The prodigy waited to get assured that the car left us. He looked at the building and said, "It is equipped with CCTV."

I looked around with too much curiosity but I didn't know how he found them. I couldn't find anything. We went behind the building. It was dark contrary to the front of the house which was lit. We took steps with difficulty. The prodigy held up his arm with the sign of stopping. Then he took out a device out of his pocket and held it towards the upper part of the entrance door. He directed the laser on it and then put it again in his pocket.

He said, "There was just one CCTV."

Then he pointed at me and said, "Give me a leg up."

I stood by the wall and gave him a leg up in order that he could climb the wall. It was difficult to climb the wall with those long cloches. Then it was Jones's turn and in following they took my hands and pulled me up. We entered the yard behind the building. The entrance door behind the building was big and unlocked. We entered. It had a big hall and the house stayed in silence. As if he knew where he was going, the prodigy moved towards a door and opened it. There was a small corridor which terminated a big room. A man's voice as well as some women's voices was heard. I hid behind the wall of the corridor and the prodigy kept on going forward. Nobody noticed us. As the prodigy kept on going, he aimed his Colt at them.

He said, "Hi Mr. Sheikh."

Sheikh jumped out of his place and the women left him while they were screaming. They were all frightened. Sheikh said things in Arabic while he was yelling.

The prodigy put his finger on his nose and said, "Hush!"

Sheikh became silent and the women looked with full astonishment. The prodigy gestured the women to get down the bed and stand in the corner of the room. Sheikh was sitting while he was gasping and his big stomach was moving up and down while he was breathing. The prodigy went towards the chair by the wall. He didn't notice that Sheikh was moving his hand under the pillow and at that time I shot his pillow. Sheikh removed his hand and the released feathers from the pillow stitched to his beard that made his figure funny. He noticed me right at that time. He looked at me and I pointed to the Colt silencer and said, "Hush!"

The prodigy put the chair in front of his bed while he was smiling at him and sat on it.

He said, "Well Mr. Sheikh, tell us..."

Sheikh said things in Arabic. The prodigy said again, "look! Please Mr. Sheik...don't play an act for me. It is better to talk in your mother language. The sweet English language I mean...business language...money language."

Sheikh's eyes opened wider. Now I got that why the prodigy called him Mr. Sheikh. The prodigy went on, "Forty years living in Saudi Arabia for England interests! You English spies are really praiseworthy in your job. I think you outdid the well-known Mr. Hempher. So there was a reason that I couldn't find the slaughterer of children and the reason is that the key factor is an originally English guy who plays the role of an Arab Sheikh. Your remembrances must be readable. It must be interesting how you come here at age of twenty and play the role of an Arab. Look Mr. Sheikh, I know you well. Now are you still going to playact an Arab Sheikh?"

While he was staring at the prodigy with no movement, Sheikh said, "Ok, assume that you have found me."

The prodigy interrupted him and said, "I assume!? It is good that you opened your mouth. But repeat your words again; what did you say? Do I assume that I found you? Oh Mr. Sheikh, look, being away from your homeland might deteriorate your English. I don't assume that I found you. You are in front of me right now and the bullet in the Colt is waiting to disintegrate your brain on your cute bed."

The prodigy looked at the women and said, "It seems there have been many things that you haven't learned them right from Muslims. It is right that you are permitted to have four wives at the same time in Saudi Arabia but it isn't right that you have all of them naked on one bed. Oh, you might have a liking to gimmick the English James Bond. But as far as I can remember James Bond might also sleep with many women but not with four women on one bed."

Sheikh was speechless about one minute and it was clear that he made him angry by his talks.

He finally said, "Well, tell me what you want?"

The prodigy said, "Look, I am waiting for you to talk, Mr. Sheikh. You are an interesting character to me. Provoking the Arab hardliners in 1978 and seizing Kaaba forcc two weeks simultaneous with the Iranian revolution was very interesting. Arabs seriously jumped out of skin. Your plan was very good. The simultaneousness of the seizing of Kaaba with the entrance of Imam Khomeini to Iran and the termination of Iran's kingdom pushes one to think that there has been a plan for it. There was going to be a peerless bloodshed but the French commandoes ruined your plan. Those poor guys didn't know that you toiled a lot to launch another Islamic brother-slaughtering. Of course brother-slaughtering took place but not as expansive as you expected and then you needed a nut for your aim that Saddam was a good choice. And hatred to Iranians was a good excuse for the start of a full-scale war and after the abortive seizure of Mecca, you encouraged Arabs to back Saddam to impede Khomeini's anti-monarchy thoughts..."

Sheikh puffed his cheeks and said, "Did you come here teach history little boy! You can't do anything damn."

The prodigy said, "No, no, no. look, don't make a mistake. It is enough to pull the trigger and I know that you know me well. Well, we never had a coincidence for a meeting but we can put up with each other."

"How?"

"Look! There is a quote that says noting can make two people intimate friends but money."

"How much?"

"You say, Mr. Sheikh."

Sheikh gulped down his saliva and said, 'I knew that you came for money but do you think I keep my money at home?"

"No Mr. Sheikh, look! I am not so much stupid. You must use your secret English account and send ten million dollars to my account."

"Is that all?"

"And of course tell me to whom did you sell the body organs?"

"I am just a connection. I sell whatsoever comes from Iran to another Arab and he gives me the whole money in return but I don't know this Arab guy."

"Look! You know him. You will not probably give the money to that stinky rich Arab to buy food for his hawks?"

"Well, it is clear now that you know everything and you just came here to kill me."

"Look! Telling the truth, I wouldn't have got so much furious if those organs had been used by those who really needed them but he is a bastard who spends all that money for his hawks' food. But I swear if you give me that money just right now, no bullet will come out of my gun."

"Well, your friend will kill me."

"I swear no bullet will come out of his gun too."

"Well, you will throttle me."

"Oh, look! I swear no one has anything to do with you; not me or anyone else in here. I swear. Send it now. Be careful not to send a code to your friends. I am not a child."

"But it isn't important how you act; they will chase you and find you anyway."

"Oh, no Mr. Sheikh! Don't worry for me. Send the money and don't worry for chasing me by my account."

The prodigy took out his cell phone and held it in front of him. While he was sending the money, one of the women started to gasp and her chest was wheezing. The other three women got embarrassed and didn't know what to do.

The prodigy looked at Sheikh and said, "Hurry Mr. Sheikh. One of your wives is not good."

Sheikh said, "Tell me your account number."

The prodigy said, "Well, I know the rest of story and entered the account number himself."

I was angry with his promise. Why should he ignore a crime for ten million dollars? So what about his claims about humanitarianism?

After sending the money, he put the mobile in his pocket and said, "Look! As I told you before my friend and I don't hurt you. It is better your wives leave the room. I imprison them in a room and you are not also allowed to exit this room for half an hour until we get far from here. I promise I come to you again if you don't act as I said. Did you get what I said? So don't do something that makes me to break my promise."

Sheik nodded and told the women, in Arabic, to leave the room. We left the room. The prodigy took the women to another room and locked it. We went towards the backdoor when a woman in burka entered the building while holding the leashes of two wolves with muzzles.

Her power in controlling the hungry wolves was very strange to me. She talked with the prodigy in Arabic. The prodigy said something. The woman nodded, took off their muzzles and went towards the sheikh's room. She released the leashes and the wolves raided his room. Sheikh's yelling echoed within the building. I was worried that someone might hear the noises but it was ok. The prodigy, Jones and I left the building and went towards the front of the building where we got out of the car. I noticed a taxi which was approaching and it braked in front of us. Tony was sitting at the back seat and was looking at us who were in wet thawb.

We got into the car. Tony who was gasping by stress said, "We must come back. Just right now."

The prodigy who was sitting in front said, "Yes sir, just right now."

He said something to the driver and he looked at him with astonishment but didn't say anything.

The car entered the road again but went the different direction opposite to Mecca. After fifteen minutes driving, he said something to the driver and gestured him to get out of the road. The driver said something while shouting and moving his hands. He pulled over. The prodigy said something to the driver and told us to get out of the car.

We got out of the car and moved towards a desert within the heart of the darkness. After some minutes walking, the prodigy stopped and said, "Well! My buddies, it was a good trip. I hope you had a good time. A plane is coming here to take you to New York. It has a smart pilot and he knows where he must drop you off."

Tony grinned and said, "It seems you are drunk! Here, in middle of a desert with sand and stones; how a plane can land here and take us? I think you took a wrong direction for the airport."

Just right at that time we heard the noise of escaping of wind stream above us. A small plane was landing vertically just above our head.

It came down gently little by little and landed. Tony looked at the prodigy and asked, "Well! what a damn do you want to do by staying in here?"

The prodigy said, "I promised you that you leave here alive and kicking and I did as I promised. Here is the plane."

Tony said, "You got crazy. It seems you forgot about our great jobs."

No Tony! "I didn't forget. I haven't still finished with my job in here. Please you all leave here. Believe me I want to stay for those great jobs. Believe me. But there is no need of you in here."

"If you have more jobs, give them to other forces. Your existence is of great importance. Don't act foolish..."

"Look! I told you that no other forces of us are in here and it isn't a job that I can concede to the other forces. Believe me whatsoever I do has been planned accurately. I must also do it myself."

Tony nodded and opened his arms for the prodigy. They hugged each other. Then Jones and the prodigy hugged each other and in following he came towards me with open arms. He hugged me and whispered stealthy, look! "I think you believe in me more than the others. I appreciate for your silence and performances as I said. Be ready David! I might give you a big mission; a mission which might be the biggest one in the world. Before making your decision you must get assured that if you really want to stay with us or not. We have burdened all those troubles to gain money and the reason is we need a huge amount of money to fulfill that great job. I promise you that the great job is just for anything but humanitarianism."

I said, "I am at you service buddy as far as your missions are for humanitarianism."

He smiled and said, "Get on buddies! See you soon. Sorry for not taking a big plane for you. Just enjoy this one. I hope there would be enough seats for Tony Bear."

Episode Five

One month after leaving Saudi Arabia, the prodigy joined us. He didn't talk too much and concentrated on our plans which I didn't know anything about. He sometimes came towards me to say something and then ignored it and turned back. I didn't also say anything and just was waiting for him to open his mouth and say what a damn wrong was with him. Tony and Jones said that they had never found him like that before. The prodigy sometimes found Liza alone and talked with her but we didn't know what they were talking about. Jones also tried to make Liza talk about the prodigy's plans but Liza answered that he would tell you everything whenever he would want.

Finally the due day came. We all five sat together and the prodigy said, "Look, I want to tell you about a significant plan."

He remained speechless for some moments. Tony said, "Hey ape! I don't wait anymore for you to drag your feet for saying that."

The prodigy said, "I hesitate because I doubt if you back me."

Jones said, "We have always been on your side except in one case that you knew about Bin Laden's place but you didn't talk about it. It was a big mistake and you might put us into trouble"

The prodigy said, "I didn't want to hide the issue. Everything must be said at its appropriate time and now I am going to talk about the very issue right now, Bin Laden's assassination."

Tony asked, "By whom? Where?"

Jones asked, "And how?"

As if the issue was too important to Toney, he got a cigar, lighted it and waited for the answer.

Liza answered, "By us and in his hide-out. And the prodigy is going to depict you how we must do it."

The prodigy explained the way that the operation had to take place and they were all talking about someone who could handle the whole operation individually in his best shape and they all reached the conclusion that they guy who was suitable for that purpose was...me.

Me! Bin Laden! Assassination! An individually operation! It was more like a joke that I was appointed to do individually the job of many giant countries which had been after it for about ten years. With regards to this issue that CIA knew that where he was hidden and didn't want to do something about that until the appropriate time so it was an extremely difficult job for me. I had to pass over CIA's and Bin Laden's protectors' barriers but could such a plan take place and especially in an individually operation.

Tony said that he had an influencer in Al Qaeda's forces so the prodigy could trace Bin Laden in that way. The prodigy accepted the protection and exit of Bin Laden's family in order to find Bin Laden's hide-out.

But why me? Why such a significant mission had to be given to me? As they said before, they had the most professional forces in their organization so why me? And why Bin Laden? There were many people in this world that had killed people ten times more than Bin Laden and they were on priority to be cleared out. I asked many questions that made the prodigy open his mouth and talk more than ever.

He started, look! You asked many questions so wait to hear the answers.

USA and Russia shit the world with their damn cold war. First the north and south Vietnam war was launched. Each of them had to have their separate play and show off their power. But then they reached the conclusion that the Middle East was the best place to continue their war. When Russia attacked Afghanistan, the USA didn't dare to counter them until a guy came out of the blue by whom the USA entered into war with Russia indirectly and it was nobody but Bin Laden. The issue that you are so dogmatic about your religion and beliefs and ignore your aristocratic living to fight for them can be regarded as huge action. Bin Laden went to Afghanistan and took many combatants from different countries. He had three hundred combatants in war with Russia according to some statistics. It was a great job by regarding the condition of that time for attracting forces.

Look! But Bin Laden did it. Of course simultaneous with the movement of Russia towards Afghanistan, Americans started their own play. They needed a fool guy to control the key point of the Middle East...I mean Iran and that fool guy was nobody but Saddam. The plays were started simultaneously; Russia's attack to Afghanistan and the Americans and Saudi Arabia's attack in the framework of Iraq to Iran.

The Americans who were freighted by Russia's influence into Afghanistan were defeated as Saddam's peerless attack for occupying Iran which was supposed to take place in two days went to nowhere. The Americans knew that they had to play in both sides. They backed Iraqis on one hand and backed Bin Laden and Mujahidin on the other hand. Bin Laden never took help from the Americans because he regarded them as his enemy so the USA gave the heavy arms to Bin Laden and Mujahidin via the Arabian countries. Russia who didn't expect such a resistance in Afghanistan failed in both the scene of war as well as the country's internal protests.

Look! The Americans wondered what to do about their plan for waging war between Iran and Iraq. Anyway Russia withdrew and the Afghan Mujahidin regarded that due to their resistance but some believe that they are wrong and Russia withdrew herself. But with no doubt if it hadn't been the Mujahidin's and Bin Laden's resistance, Russia would never have withdrawn. Then Russia sat and watched the play between Iran and Iraq. Of course both USA and Russia were doing their best to seize Iran when Iran's king left the country. Russia was trying to inject the communistic beliefs in the Iranian thoughts and culture and the USA was after Iran oil industry.

But they never thought that the presence of Khomeini ruined drastically all their plans. The communists disappeared and the Americans also couldn't succeed to seize oil. None of them also dare to have any direct action against Iran so the USA continued its play with Saddam and Russia with the domestic conflicts in Iran – both in the hope of seizing this country.

In the wake of Russia's withdrawal from Afghanistan, the Americans decided to instigate Bin Laden to attack Iran from the east. But Bin Laden wasn't someone whom they could make him get into their plays. While the Americans were planning such a scheme, Bin Laden was requested to return to Saudi Arabia by the government and his family and he did. The result of the skirmishes over Afghanistan was domestic conflicts that continued for years but in fact the other countries ignited that war.

On the other hand Saddam gave up due to the Iranians' resistance. So the play of the west and the east was nearly over and they had to think of another scheme for the sequel of the play. Now for using the weapons, another excuse had to be made. The Americans spent billions of dollars for Iran-Iraq war and it went to nowhere. A hero like Bin Laden was also a threat for the US as he was a dogmatic Islamist and also anti-US. On the other hand the US failed to gain the brilliant center stone of the world, Iran whose old rich culture had, in comparison with their two hundred years of culture, always been an obsession for them. Now the Americans who found that they couldn't proceed without their own presence in the region, they launched the wildest dance of the history. They planned a play and the play was that the anti-US Bin Laden had to take measures against America in order to come back to the Middle East again. Then when everything would look logical why wouldn't the US accuse Saddam with using atomic and chemical bombs, in order to control both sides of Iran for a full-scale attack? Isn't it right? So Bin Laden, the twin towers and displaying the US as an oppressed nation altogether was a good plan and then Russia, the new formed of the Soviet Union was waiting to see how the play would go on.

I asked, "It means you believe that it wasn't Bin Laden who ordered the eleven September attack?"

The prodigy said, "Look! I don't talk about my beliefs. What I say is according to the documentaries. No doubt that one side of that attack was Bin Laden. Many people say the eleven September operation took place by the Mujahidin under the surveillance of Bin Laden but not by his order. Whenever he was asked if they killed people in war against America, he answered, "No, "That is another issue. We have nothing to do with ordinary people." He rejected with anger many times all terroristic operations which were planned for killing people in occupied places and threatened he would punish the relative element if it would happen. The eleven September event wasn't directly planed by Bin Laden but later he found himself in a happening that he was recognized guilty for it. He didn't censure about it but he didn't also take the responsibility of the event.

The issue that the security system of America was disturbed in a given day and time and that such a terrorist attack took place easily was laughter-provoking. Exactly in the same day all Jewish staff of that world trade organization took a leave for off time. The issue that two famous and significant towers with thousands of people disappear might be of no importance for a politician but it is too excellent for the global attraction.

So the US had to come back to the first world scene...Bin Laden for Afghanistan and Saddam for Iraq. But both those countries' plays didn't take too much time in the region so the two aces Bin Laden and Saddam had to be remained hidden until the presence of the Americans to be continued in the region. But we ruined the first ace and killed Saddam whom was kept captive by themselves and made the Americans to spend a lot of money to make documents for his assassination. So the Americans who wanted to be seemed as a hero had to pull out a fabricated Saddam from a hole. So they televised him and showed some films which identified him to tell the world that they found and arrested the real Saddam and saved people's lives out of that bloodthirsty dictator...a play and then the hanging. Their first play who was Saddam encountered failure but about their second play; it had to be a different one that could succeed to cheat people and this time Bin Laden had to be kept hidden in a way that to raise more significant challenges. Saddam was hidden under severe security measures which didn't work well so they had to scheme a new plan for hiding Bin Laden and they really did it. If you want to hide a precious diamond, you must not put it in a glassy box which is visible to everyone even with best security measures so it is better to keep it mixed with the other crystal pieces like the ones resembling those in your house's chandelier and it was weird that they did it. While it was easy for them to find Bin Laden, they led him indirectly to a place where he seemed apparently hidden."

The prodigy looked at me and I was staring at him with my hands crossed on my chest. He looked at me for some moments and said, "Look, if you don't believe me, let me show you something. Look at the display of laptop; what do you see? What you see is a mosquito...yes. Now let me zoom on it...now I think you are doubtful about it. Now let me zoom more...yes it is an electronic mosquito at the same size and dimensions of a normal mosquito. It was designed in 2000. If you give it a human DNA, it will find them whenever they are in this world. So can all those ten years of investigating for finding Bin Laden be anything but a ridiculous play for the world?

Now Bin Laden...you tell me. You know everything better than me. Let's assume that just Bin Laden was the key factor for collapsing of the twin towers and doing the other terrorist attacks. How many people were killed? About three thousand people ultimately. Now let's go back to the question which you asked me many times. How many people were killed by the US and England for finding someone who had killed three thousand people in Afghanistan and Iraq?

Look David, you told me about your thoughts and plans and the way you looked at the UN before and the way you look now. Is the issue that someone is a threat for the world a good excuse for the massacre of thousands of people in the world and shouldn't the UN prevent it? There were a lot of humanitarian and voluntary actions which have been taken place with the name of the UN but they were all plays by which the UN has been responsible for the bloodshed of millions of people.

Look, let's review the history once more. The UN's neglecting in 1991 led to the death of two million people in Rwanda. The UN's interference in Congo's resolution and preventing it to be put into effect also led to the death of five million people. Seven million people have been killed just in the two events except from millions of people whom are killed all over the whole world within the wars which have been waged by the US and Russia. Just compare their toll rate with Bin Laden's three thousands. And I say again that he never accepted the charge of those massacres. As far as I know Bin Laden plan was attacking to Pentagon. He always said, "Our war is with US's military forces, not people." The mission of attacking the twin towers was supposed to be given to Bin Laden in 1996 but he didn't accept it. Even before eleven September, there was once more another attack to the twin towers that wasn't successful and had no concern with him too.

Look, it is good to know that Bin Laden's criminal file is cleared of any charges concerning the twin towers and he is chased due to the terroristic attacks which took place in some Arabian countries against the US. It was good for the west to continue the play for an attack and Khalid sheikh Mohammad who was supposed just to get the mission of attacking to Pentagon found the opportunity to put the charge on Bin Laden. Khalid sheikh Mohammad's scheme for attacking the twin towers was so foolish that couldn't take place in a country such as America but when the government wants it to be done, why not?

When you know that something is going to be done which will be a good excuse for your aims, why should you hurdle it? So they added fuel to the fire to show themselves innocent. Now the poor Americans have been attacked. It is enough that the enemy's bomb makes more sounds then everyone forgets to compare the toll rate of the enemy's bomb with the toll rate of the Americans' bomb. Yes, I found that where he was but I didn't take any measure. David, I agree with you that if we are going to take a measure, there are more cases on priority. If I tell you that you must kill Bin Laden, it is not for his charges or ruining the American's play. After arresting Bin Laden, he is going to be interviewed and he might say many things that ruin the feature of Islam in order to launch another world war – a war in which people kill all Muslims and the non-Muslim countries are let to attack Muslim countries to launch another bi-polar world war.

So kill Bin Laden! Kill him to prevent a global massacre. Kill him to prevent the world war three."

******

From Mars I started my practices for performing the operations pertaining to the assassination of Bin Laden and I had a strange feeling for doing the most important killing of the world.

I always used to do things which were on priority in my life and by considering the priority, I preferred to kill those who caused to create people like Bin Laden and caused the killing of millions of people.

But the prodigy insisted on killing Bin Laden first as the lives of millions of people were in dander due to the play that they schemed. Now I was able to ruin the global massacre scheme.

Despite of being a commando, what I was going to do in the operation was something new and strange.

I had to be equipped with a capsule having jet fans. It had to be attached on your back. It was equipped with metal tubes which were connected to jet fans. The jet fans had also to be attached to your upper part of your legs. The computer program was planned in a way that the jet fans would fly as soon as I would reach a place five kilometer away from Bin Laden's hideout.

In five kilometer away from Bin Laden's hideout, the jet fans had to fly me in the sky according to the given data and had to put me on the roof of his hideout. I was supposed to be equipped with a Colt, a machine gun, a night vision camera and a compass. I would ruin the whole scheme if I couldn't finish my work with the two weapons.

I had to enter the building from the backdoor after landing on a three-store building which was Bin Laden's hideout. I had to enter his room on the third floor, killing him and that was all.

The prodigy said, "No armed man is in the building. They might have weapons for self-defense but there is no bodyguard or someone like that. They have a simple life that made people of that region never think of the existence of an important individual like Bin Laden. "

It was exactly as the prodigy described. The best way for hiding a diamond is to treat it like a piece of glass in order to be seemed a common object.

It was exactly the very thing that the US was after in order to continue advancing in the region on the excuse of looking for Bin Laden. They were looking for someone they knew its place and now I was coming to ruin the play like Jones who ruined the play for Saddam. Jones wasn't suitable for doing the operation as he wasn't strong enough to bear the pressure of the jet fans. The prodigy wasn't also suitable for the operation as reaching Bin Laden wasn't an easy job so they gave the mission to me as I was a professional commando and an exceptional individual because of my strong smelling ability.

Tony bear, Jones and the prodigy continuously repeated identical words and statements about the final stage of the operation.

"As soon as you enter and see Bin Laden, don't think; shoot and come back. Think over it before you go and if you might change your mind for doing the mission, change it now. You can't change your decision while you are doing the operation."

And I changed my minds times and times. I made a decision and changed it again. I became decisive again and changed my mind again. While I was entangled in all those mental skirmishes, I remembered Sara that asked me once, "You could be an engineer, a doctor or a specialist in any other job; why did you enter army?"

I answered, "I could be many other things but I decided to be in a position where I can save more people's lives. A doctor or an engineer might save just some lives in a year but I can save thousands or millions of lives."

The operation could save millions of lives. I shouldn't have thought about him. I shouldn't have thought about this issue that he had no intention for killing people. I shouldn't have thought that if he valued his family or not or how he behaved his children as a father. I shouldn't have thought about this issue that why he left his aristocratic living and went to the mountains and deserts to fight. I should have thought about this issue that killing him will prevent the killing of millions of people. The prodigy was right. There was still no charge of attacking the twin towers in his criminal file and he was chased for the other charges.

When you have a deep look at the event, you ask yourself; how do we know that he was responsible for those assassinations? Why are there people like Bin Laden in this world? Why should someone leave his aristocratic living and go to fight? No, I shouldn't have thought about those things.

When I watched some films of Bin Laden in which he confessed his terrorist attacks, I easily recognized that the guy in the films wasn't the real Bin Laden but how can you make people understand things like this? People get the news from the media. The media that tell lies and people believe them regardless to this issue that who controls those media. I should have thought. I shouldn't have thought. I shouldn't have thought at the time that I should have thought. I didn't know what to do. It was the first time that I should have thought what to do in the operation I was given. But in my previous operations, I just thought how to perform the operation that was planned for me and what a conspiracy I found when I was performing the T2 operation. There might be less war in this world if the soldiers were permitted to act based on their deliberations. I didn't like anymore to be a soldier. I didn't like others to order me and I obey them. I didn't trust anyone and any organization and now I was entangled in an event which didn't have any specific shape. The only thing that the prodigy was after and seemed ridiculous was that he intended to launch a foundation that to impede war and blood shedding in the world...a real United Nation Organization...an organization that defends the oppressed people not the governments' interests. He wanted to have an army as expansive as the whole world in order to fix up anyone who wanted to launch war in the very beginning of their measure. He wanted to launch an organization that to impede the shooting of just even one missile...an organization that didn't let the governments decide for its people and let people decide for themselves.

When I asked him, "Where must you start?" He answered, "First we must find the writers and directors of those ridiculous plays."

He said that all we saw on the top of the governments were just the players and the writers, and the directors of the plays would never reveal themselves. He said that Killing the players was so easy and wasn't an impediment in advancing the work because a director could substitute another player.

His main aim was that he wanted to ruin the shows in front of the TV cameras in order to make those writers and directors reveal their real identity. By killing Saddam, he nearly reached his goal but he couldn't reach a good conclusion.

Then he was hopeful to find those show-makers by the play that they made for Bin Laden...the show-makers who had the control of the media, power and money.

I was bored of this complicated world, horror and killing. Since Sara left me, I imagine myself with her in a green land in my dreams. With hair flying with the wind, I always see her smile and hop like a small girl. I see her who dance with our not-borne children, laugh and scream happily. I go towards her, hug her and kiss her. Our children play with us naughtily and...why shouldn't this world be like this? Damn to war and weapon.

I made my decision not for killing someone who there was no real official document for his charges but for ruining that ridiculous play and saving millions lives. Sometimes I thought of myself, "I assume that I ruin this one; what about the next? They can easily make another Bin Laden; it isn't a difficult task."

The prodigy said, "Don't worry about these things. I have stolen so many documents from CIA that I will reveal them if they want to deny Bin Laden's assassination."

But I knew that those documents could be effective for just some years to shut up the mouth of a government. Once the governors might come in front of the cameras and confess with flagrancy, "The attack to the twin towers was our work to prevent the annihilation of the whole country and we are happy to save your lives. We hope you forgive us for that event and want you to consider the issue that some people died but millions are still alive."

And the fool people would think, "Yes, they are right. It is right that three thousands were killed but millions of people are still alive."

They say those words to make people not to think about the issue that millions of lives have been claimed under the pretext of the death of three thousand people in twin tower attack. But as far as I think my life is different with other lives and consider my life valuable but the other lives just as a media record, we can't claim we are human beings.

Abutaleb always said, "My son, we aren't always responsible for what we do. We are sometimes responsible for what we don't do. Sometimes our silence and nonchalance towards a catastrophe is more disgraceful than the catastrophe itself because when we aren't silent or nonchalant, we can prevent the catastrophe to take place or not to be repeated at least. I didn't obey Saddam's order to fight with the Iranians and I did a right thing. I had a share to terminate the war and I did it. My share was to disobey the order and I did my best. We must prove our humanity to God, not to the Governors. What is right to do is to stand obedient to God, not to stand against my religious brothers. No, you must have a reason for killing a man. When you kill someone, you must have an admissible reason for it because you are judged before the Lord. For example you killed someone because you know if you hadn't killed him, he would have killed you and others. But we had no reason for killing the Iranians. They didn't attack us. They had nothing wrong to do with the other countries. Iran's king helped the Arab nations many times for many years. And if he hadn't helped us, we might have died out of hunger. Khomeini didn't also want war with any country and if there was a war it was domestic conflicts. But the Arab nations protected Saddam for defeating the powerful Iran."

I made my decision to do my mission but they changed the time of the operation. We were supposed to do it in the end of May but the prodigy suddenly changed his mind and said, "Now or never."

We moved from New York at four in the afternoon by a vertical take-off and landing jet. It was just the prodigy and I. I was angry with the change of the operation time. He was also angry. When I asked him why he changed the time, he answered, "The Americans send their forces to arrest Bin Laden at midnight but they don't want to announce it until the due time. I don't know why they made such a decision."

I asked, "Might our plan have been betrayed?"

He answered, "I don't know but we must ruin the play. The fable of Bin Laden must be over tonight before they come and arrest him."

According to the plan, we landed on a hill five kilometers away from Eibat-Abad. The prodigy told that everything was under the precise surveillance of the Americans from that distance. But my jet fans weren't traceable. I put on the special cloth. I put the fuel cylinder on my back which was very heavy and fastened the jet fans to my legs. I put the 20 centimeter Toto machine gun and the Toti Colt which were both made by the prodigy, on my stomach. I had never seen weapons like those ones before. The Toto machine gun was just a bit bigger than a normal Colt which had the capacity of fifty tiny poisonous bullets and the Colt had three bullets. It was professional and perfect. I had to kill Bin Laden by the three bullets of the Colt. He gave the Colt to me and said, "Shoot his head not his heart. Did you get? Just the head."

I wanted to ask him why but he interrupted me and said, "Don't ask any question. I have no answer for it now. Just shoot his head...just his head."

He gave a piece of cloth to me and said, "Smell it. This is Bin Laden's body odor. When you enter the building, you can find him easier by knowing the smell."

I took the cloth and smelled it. It had a strange smell. I had never smelled an odor like that before and I kept it in my mind.

I put the special flying helmet on my head and put my arms crossed on my chest. Three...two...one...I jumped out of the ground for five kilometers flying. The jet fans had no sound or light reflection. I was just like a ghost which was moving in the heart of the night. As I practiced before, my flight would take just sixty and three seconds. I landed on the roof of the three-story building. I could clearly hear the sound of my heart beating. I took off the cylinder and the jet fans. I moved towards the door of the roof. I heard the prodigy's voice.

"From C to A...from C to A"

"A is speaking. I, roof, roger."

"Two helicopters...towards the south of the west north...two hundred meters.

I checked the compass and turned towards west north south. I removed the face protector but I didn't see anything. I looked around. There was no sound and no movement.

"No, there is a mistake."

"No, look! Listen to me. The helicopters are with no sound and light exactly like the jet fans."

"What must I do?"

There was no answer. It was disconnection.

I said again, "From A to C...from A to C. I can't hear you."

A sound like parasite came out of my phone that I found our connection was traced. I turned on the binocular of my helmet. He was right. Two helicopters were approaching like ghosts with no sound. What should I have done? The operation was disturbed. I had to think it over. As a commando, my common sense told me one of them would go up to the roof and the other would go down.

I had no time and I had to do something. I took out the machine gun and shot. I shot the back propeller of one of the helicopters and there was a smoke out of it. The second helicopter suddenly changed its direction and moved away. The first helicopter went towards the yard of the building.

Its tail hit the wall of the yard and its fuselage smashed the ground with a huge explosion in a way that its tail was separated. I entered the building from the roof door. Some moments later I heard the sound of shooting. I also heard some people who were talking in both Arabic and American. I had to focus on my aim...I...third floor...Bin Laden's odor. I found the room. I kicked it. The door opened. Bin Laden...prayer rug....a woman in burka beside him...his smile.

"You are welcome my brother."

Shooting, shooting and shooting...it was over.

There was hustle and bustle in the whole building. I got out of the roof door. I looked at the yard stealthy from the edge of the roof. The second helicopter landed in the yard too.

Someone shouted, "The roof."

I jumped back and stood in the middle of the roof. I put the fuel cylinder on my back and the jet fans on my legs. The computerized program of the jet fans was disturbed. I pressed the bottoms but they didn't work.

"From A to C...from A to C...I have no connection...from A to C.

I heard the unpleasant sound from my phone again.

"No connection...no connection damn!"

His voice was clear for a moment.

"Stand for flying."

I stood upright with arms crossed on my chest. Three...two...one...and I was in the sky. I felt like a spirit who was going to the heaven. I wasn't cold or hot. I wasn't happy or sad. I had no feeling. I noticed that my flight took longer time. First I thought I was wrong. I flied more time up to about five minutes with high speed. Then the jet fans' speed reduced and I landed on a tree. I thought they didn't work well. I flied from a place that had no tree and now I landed among a mass of trees. A tree branch pierced within the gap between the cylinder and my waist and scratched my waist. I released the cylinder and the jet fans. I climbed down the tree. The night vision camera was on. I noticed someone. I felt the prodigy's odor but I took out the machine gun. He opened his arms and said, it was fantastic Mr. A...fantastic.

When I heard his voice, I got calm.

Then he started clapping and said," It was so excellent that I can't find a suitable word in praising your work."

I asked, "Why was it disconnected damn guy?"

They found our link and I had to hack the Pentagon's connection in order to connect you through their signals. Well, it wasn't an easy job. It took a little bit time. I found that Bin Laden was killed through their messages. I hope your camera has recorded everything well. I removed the camera from my helmet and gave it to him. He connected one head of a wire to the camera and the other head to his mobile cellphone. All images and the sound were clear.

He said, look! It was a pity that I couldn't watch them at the scene.

He opened one arm and put the other hand on his chest. He bent and said, "I must bow you."

I killed Bin Laden but many things surely took place within the very two seconds and just the prodigy knew what happened.

******

Jones says, "Come on David. Come and see what a new play these rascals have schemed!"

I say, "What are you talking about?"

Jones says, "TV news...let me turn it up."

I enter the room. Now I can hear it clearly. I am staring at the TV with my hands on my waist.

"Robert O'Neal the ex-commando who was in Pakistan for participating in the mission concerning killing the ex-leader of Al-Qaeda said to Washington Post in a new interview that it was his shot that killed Bin Laden.

His claim defies Matt Bissonnette's utterance. Matt Bissonnette is the other commando who took part at the same mission. In a book in 2012, he claimed that Bin Laden was killed by his shot."

I say, "Please shut it up. What do you think about the new play that they have schemed?"

Jones says, "Well, you damn guy, they are afraid of us. The United States paid through the nose and a heavy price for what you did. US planned this scheme by his best writers and intellectuals and then you shit the biggest and most costly scenario of the history. You changed that historical scenario. They want to pull us out of our closet by the new claims through the reports and media or they want just to say that it has been a repeated unreal claim by many nuts if we reveal the truth once."

It has been a long time that something inside me has been titillating my curiosity to ask this question and just Jones knows the answer to this question. So I ask, "Was killing Saddam enjoyable for you?"

Jones says, "I have never enjoyed killing. Never, even Saddam. But I have no doubt that I did right."

I say, "In fact you ruined their plan so they made that ridiculous televised hanging."

Jones says, "Not important. We must do our job. Then they can scheme any plan they wish. What is of high importance is that we ruined the key play."

Tony Bear says, "Hey you damn bastards! I also killed Gaddafi, but I don't disturb other people's sleeping. Shit your bed and shut your eyes. We have a big job tomorrow; a bigger job than killing Bin Laden, Saddam and Gaddafi. So shut up."

I faced the prodigy. After many months in the wake of Bin Laden's operation, I had still many questions which were left with no answer. I noticed his look which was different.

He asked, "Well! Ask now."

I asked, why did you insist that I shot his head? When I opened the door and entered the room, he said, "You are welcome my brother. Why did he say that? Why was his wife in burka in his private room?"

The prodigy closed his eyes for some moments. First I thought he was going to skip my questions. Then he opened his eyes, smiled and answered, "Because he planned his assassination operation himself and we just performed it. He didn't like to be killed by shot in his heart. That was all."

He got up and went towards his bag. He brought out some notes out of it and put them in front of me.

Two thousand and one hundred and twenty dollars; it was all his belongings and told me to give it to the guy who would kill him. He didn't like to owe anyone after his death.

I was just looking at him. I didn't know what to do or what to say. He could understand how I felt with no doubt.

He continued, look! I think like you David. I think about this issue that why we had to kill him.

Why don't we smash the heads of those who are the cause of millions of people's massacre? Like some those dirty guys who are in the United Nations? First I decided to convince Bin Laden to hide somewhere in order not to be found by the Americans but he didn't accept what I said. I told him that I found him through the Americans channel but he couldn't believe me.

He said, "If you can prove that the Americans know my place, it means that they betrayed me again and I have experienced so many betrayals like this one that makes me feel I don't want to be alive anymore."

The prodigy got up, kept my shoulder and said, "When I sent him the documents and let him find that there was conspiracy against him, he found that his arresting would have aftereffects in return. If he had been killed by the other guys, there would have been no document that proved his assassination and another Bin Laden might be created. He also wanted us to kill him because suicide is haram in Islam.

By the way, how do you feel now? What do you think about me now? What do you think about what I told you? You might think that I am a lunatic liar. It is exactly right. I am a lunatic liar. But as Pablo Picasso said, "Art is the lie that enables us to realize the truth."